Date Due

FEB 8			
APR 1 0			
OCT 13			
OCT 2 2			
MAR 1 7			
MAR 1 5 2005			
	PRINTED IN U. S. A.		

THE MAN FROM
ROCCA SICCA

The Man from Rocca Sicca

By

REGINALD M. COFFEY, O.P.

THE BRUCE PUBLISHING COMPANY
MILWAUKEE

Nihil obstat: James M. Egan, O.P., S.T.D.
Philip F. Mulhern, O.P., S.T.D.
Imprimi potest: Terence S. McDermott, O.P., S.T.Lr.,
Prior Provincial
Imprimatur: ✠ Michael J. Curley, D.D.,
Archbishop of Baltimore and Washington

September 30, 1942

War Format

Departures from the usual Bruce style in the format of this book are the result of necessary war conservation of materials and labor. In every respect, however, the book is complete and unabridged.

MARIAE, SEDI SAPIENTIAE

Preface

THE ordinary reader of an ordinary book necessarily takes advantage of the author. Like an eavesdropper or a keyhole peeper, he is given the intimate view normally proper to long acquaintance or close friendship without paying the price of affection usually exacted for passage of the tollgate of a human soul. If it weren't that the author had brought it on himself, it would be decidedly unfair for this intimate knowledge needs sympathetic reception; it is all right for God who loves us infinitely, and for our friends who love us tolerantly, but it is much too sharp a sword to put into the hands of those who not only do not love us, but do not even know us.

Of course, it might be argued, such self-revelation as necessarily goes into a book also works to the author's advantage. Often enough he wins friends he has never seen and will never hear from; and this rich harvest of affection has been reaped with none of the labor and sacrifice which are the usual price of love. Even so, the author is still at a disadvantage at having little or nothing to say about the list of his friends as well as of his relations. The reader has some grounds for complaint, for to get the message carried by the book he is forced into the role of eavesdropper or keyhole peeper, a role unpleasant to most men capable of reading books.

The danger and unpleasantness of this personal revelation is faced frankly by an author because the meat of book he is writing is, in his opinion, an essential of the diet of men.

That it be offered to men is, in his opinion, much more important than anything the public may think or discover about the author as a man. Where this is not the case, we have an author suffering insufferable conceit and readers suffering insufferable books.

St. Thomas Aquinas underwent a distinctively different penalty in authoring his great works. The massive splendor and intrinsic beauty of his incredible literary output have almost completely hidden Thomas Aquinas, the man. Perhaps he would have had it so. After all, he was a saint, strong in humility, entranced by the beauty of God and astonished that his own insignificance should attract so much divine attention. Then, too, the matter of his greatest work — the whole field of truth about God, man, the world, and the Saviour of the world — caught the eyes of men and held them so fixed there was not time for so much as a glimpse at the author behind the splendid array of eternal truths. He himself had written to meet great crises, at top speed, with death crowding his plans, with the men of all succeeding generations depending on the accuracy of every stroke of his pen. Even without his saintly obliteration of himself, men would have been hard pressed to comprehend his message and still have time to trace the dim outline of the author on the crowded pages.

It is true that not even such a man as Thomas should get between the eyes of men and the matter and goals of which he wrote. Still, such complete concealment of the author as history has shown in the works of Thomas gave those works a kind of anonymity. And this, as events have shown, is very bad indeed.

Thus, his works can be, and have been, treated like anonymous letters; tossed in the wastebasket by ages terribly busy with works whose authors' great names were scrawled on every page. Or they can be looked at with an impersonal detachment, as though a human heart, a human mind, and human strength had not been poured into them at the cost of life pouring out of the author, nor a precise slant and shadow painstakingly given to every word in the works. One could almost think these things were dead and treat them mercilessly; or look upon them as a collection of disembodied words, empty vessels into which any meaning could be poured at a reader's pleasure. As quasianonymous, the works of Thomas could be twisted and turned to fit the quirks of an age, since it was presumed that the intelligence directing those works, co-ordinating their parts, is an unknown quantity safely disregarded.

In other words, the apparent anonymity of Thomas' labors is a serious injustice. It is an injustice to Thomas who deserves much more of the men for whom he labored every instant of his life and whom he defended against all enemies. It is an injustice to his work, allowing it to be more easily misunderstood, its hidden riches more surely left untouched, its supernatural sublimity — the product of sanctity, prayer, and divinely aided labor — more surely hidden. It is an injustice to the men who read the works of Thomas, robbing them of such a patiently understanding friend as Thomas, keeping them from an intimacy with one who had so much to give those who dared to approach closely to him.

Father Coffey's book makes some amends to Thomas, his works, and his readers by concentrating on Thomas the man. Much has been written about the works of Thomas; probably too much. Much has been done to the works of Thomas; certainly too much. Not nearly enough has been said of Thomas himself. The thing is probably understandable enough. After all, Thomas gathered up the wisdom of the ancients of the East and the West, assimilated all the discoveries and hints of discoveries that came out of the thousand years that went into the making of scholasticism, sent his mind out into the clashing intellectual battles of his own brilliant age at the first sound of the battle trumpet and handed all this plus his own genius on to succeeding ages in the supreme philosophical and theological writings that have come from Christendom. Men might easily have been overwhelmed by his work. Or, having braved the story of the work, have been in such awe of such a man as to have feared to approach him.

The men of his own Dominican family, however, have known him through the hundreds of years as the quiet, friendly, unassuming brother whose genius had to be discovered by accident, and whose thoughtful help of the stumbling beginner could be interrupted only by death. We have known him as understanding, marvelously patient, and very wise. A man, surely, well worth the knowing.

The men of our time particularly need the friendship of just such a man. For our age desperately needs a strong, capable friend of men; a more magnificent defense of humanity than Thomas' has never been penned. Our age needs a cosmopolitan view of eternity and the world to escape the provincialism that is already blinding us even to the world; few men have seen as deeply into eternity or as profoundly into the confusing details of the world's perfect order. Above all our age needs an articulate lover of God, one who can say the ineffable things that set our hearts soaring and yet leave our minds enlightened rather than obscured; no theologian has sung of God in theological prose more sweetly than Thomas.

We need Thomas as well as his works. Father Coffey has given us a humanly touching introduction to Brother Thomas.

WALTER FARRELL, O.P.,
Chaplain R. A. W. Farrell, USNR.

Contents

xi

Chapter 1

The Countess Bears a Son

THEODORA, Countess of Aquino, was heavy with child. As she sat, sunk in thought, gazing from the casement of a chamber high up in a turret of her castle, it was the child within her that occupied Theodora's thoughts. Motherhood was no new experience for the countess. She had already brought five children into the world. But never since her first pregnancy had the new life growing within her so captivated her attention. The reason why this baby so occupied its mother's waking thoughts and the dreams of her sleep was not entirely clear to Theodora. The preoccupation of her mind and imagination with her first infant was easily explainable. Then she was looking forward to and waiting for the new experience of motherhood. Now that experience had long since ceased to be a novelty. Some other explanation there must be for the bridelike anticipation of the birth of this child. Perhaps it was best explainable by the fact that so many of her hopes and dreams, so much that was important in Theodora's life, lay in the tiny hands of this undelivered child. Within its embryonic arms, close-folded on its breast as if in prayer, reposed, it seemed to her, her future happiness.

So it was that as Theodora, having dismissed her maidens, sat looking through the casement at the fertile valley far below she saw nothing of the richness of the plains that rolled away from the foot of Rocca Sicca, the crag whereon her castle perched like a bird of prey. Her mind was entirely engrossed with the tiny tenant of her womb. Would it be a boy or a girl? Another boy would evenly divide the family, another girl would make the score four to two for the spinners. As she gazed, Theodora's lips moved in silent prayer, begging God's gracious mother to grant her the favor of a boy.

Yes, Theodora hoped and prayed for a son, in spite of the fact that sons were hazards in these perilous times when wars between the Pope and the Emperor were constant. Her husband, Landulf was even now away at war fighting for his cousin, the Emperor Frederick II, against the Vicar of Christ. At his side, as esquire, rode her eldest son, Landulf, still but a boy. Her second son, Reynaldo, hardly more than a child had watched them depart with tears in his eyes. He, too, the scion of a soldier race, would be off to the wars almost before he was able to keep his seat on a prancing, pawing charger. In neither of these two boys could Theodora see an *alter Christus* and that was why she so longed that this child should be a boy. Perhaps a third son might be a priest, and if a priest surely an abbot, and if an abbot why not the Vicar of Christ.

Theodora thrilled to the ecstasy of her dream. Her head rose proudly as she pictured an Aquino upon the throne of the fisherman. Why should it not be so? In his veins would flow the best blood of Italy. Landulf had already promised her that he would make no claims upon a third son. He would not rear him to the sword and saddle. She might reserve him for the priesthood as long as he received a distinction worthy of his name, a bishopric or, better still, the abbot's throne in the ancient Monastery of Monte Cassino, near by.

In this Theodora quite agreed with her warrior spouse. It would never do for the son of the great family of the Counts of Aquino and Lords of Loreto, Acerra and Belcastro to be a common monk or priest. In fact, such an eventuality was impossible. The Holy See's ever present sense of the fitness of things would not allow such a reversal of right order. An Aquino who entered Holy Orders would, of necessity, be an abbot or a bishop.

Theodora's fancy had quite carried her away. She could already see this mite in her womb, clothed in the ancient habit of St. Benedict, with the jeweled miter of the Lord Abbot of Monte Cassino upon his noble brow. But the realization suddenly came to her, with something of a shock, that the child in her womb was still unborn; it might still be a girl and not even the power and prestige of the Aquino's could make her a priest much less lord abbot. The countess, forgetting her fierce Italian pride, once more became the devout Christian and the suppliant daughter of Mary. "O Mother of God," she prayed, "grant me a son."

She was still murmuring her prayer when one of her maidens returned to the chamber to inform her that the hermit of the neighborhood wished to have words with her. He had, said the maid, a message of the greatest import to the House of Aquino. The countess gave the maid permission to conduct the holy man to her presence. A few minutes later the maid returned followed by the wild figure of a mountain holy man.

Bonus, the solitary, would have appeared out of place in any civilized surroundings. But as he stood here amidst the luxury of a great lady's private apartment, he presented a spectacular contrast. His hair was long, sun bleached, and unkempt, his beard ragged and dirty. His craggy face, what could be seen of it, was the color of well tanned leather and was seamed and roughened by the wind and rain. His body was clothed in rough untanned skins. He wore sandals and in his hand he carried a staff.

Bonus was typical of the holy men of whom there were hundreds in the Europe of the day. Wishing to attain a closer union with God, Bonus had fled to the wilderness, where he was alone with God, and His handmaiden, Nature. His spiritual cares were provided for by the monks of Monte Cassino and the inhabitants of the region saw to it that he did not starve.

The countess had no feeling of either contempt or aversion for this eccentric. To her his strange wild appearance was not the object of derision. In common with the people of her day, the countess' attitude toward the hermit was one of respect and admiration mixed with awe. In him she saw a modern John the Baptist, to whom life was only a springboard to heaven. It would remain for the women of a later age, living material lives unto material ends, to be disgusted or frightened by such disregard, such sublime contempt for matter and material things. And so Bonus, the unkempt hermit, was a welcome visitor to the home of the highborn countess.

Bonus approached the countess with no trace of awe or embarrassment. Standing before her with burning eyes that saw before him, not a countess but only a child of Mary, he began to speak: "Rejoice, O lady, for thou art about to have a son whom thou shalt call Thomas. Thou and thy spouse will think to make him a monk in the Monastery of Monte Cassino, where the body of St. Benedict reposes, in the hope that your son will attain to the honors and riches of that monastery. But God has ordained otherwise because he will be a friar in the Order of Preachers. Such will be his learning and holiness that his equal will not be found throughout the whole world."

Having delivered his message, the hermit departed leaving Theodora to her thoughts and prayers.

Some time after this event the countess bore her son. At his baptism Pope Honorius III, represented by his proxy, the Bishop of Aquino, accepted the obligation of godfather. The baby was christened Thomas, which signifies an abyss. Never was a child more aptly named.

Chapter 2

View of the Times

SINCE every man is, in a certain sense, the product of the age in which he lives, it might be well before continuing our sketch of St. Thomas briefly to outline his times. There has been, probably, no period in the history of the world that has been more subject to dispute. To the anti-Catholic historian, it is one of the most lamentable periods since the world's beginning. To him it falls in the category that has been conveniently labeled "the dark ages" in contradistinction to "the light ages" which begin at the "Reformation." It is the epitome of all that is degrading to human dignity, an age when ignorance and superstition held sway. This extreme partisan view is today held by no one who pretends to scholarship.

Catholic scholars have labeled this period the age of Faith and the century in which Thomas was born has been called "the greatest of centuries." And, since pithy slogans are much more convenient than numerous details, Catholics are inclined to consider this period, when there was but one fold and one shepherd in the western world, as a near approach to an earthly paradise.

As is usually the case neither extreme view is correct. The same forces of evil that produced the revolt of Luther and the defection of a good part of Europe from the fold of Christ were at work then. A Luther was possible in the sixteenth century because by that time the secular power had become predominant. He was not possible in the thirteenth because then the Popes held the upper hand.

But the attack that was to rob the Popes of their ascendancy had already been launched. Sporadic and feeble attempts had been made before but the Pope had always triumphed. Henry IV, clad in sackcloth and standing barefoot in the snow at Canossa is symbolic of the outcome of all these early encroachments upon the power of the Holy See.

The final drive against papal supremacy and a drive which resulted in ultimate victory was inaugurated by the German king and Holy Roman Emperor, Frederick I, nicknamed Barbarossa because of his flaming red beard. Barbarossa, who, incidentally, was the great-uncle of Thomas Aquinas and whose armies were commanded by Thomas' grandfather (also called Thomas), hurled his legions against the Pope. Although the Pope emerged victorious from his clash with Frederick, he suffered a moral defeat; for Frederick was never suitably punished.

Frederick's son, Henry VI, continued his father's policy of opposition to the Papal power but since he was not a strong ruler, he did not make a great deal of headway. It remained for his son, Frederick II, a cousin of St. Thomas to become a real thorn in the Pope's side. While both Barbarossa and Henry VI were antagonistic to the Pope as a temporal ruler, they never challenged his spiritual authority. Frederick II denied the authority of the Pope in both the spiritual and temporal orders.

Frederick II was a perverted genius. In intellectual ability and the universal character of his interests he bears a striking resemblance to his cousin from Rocca Sicca. A patron of the arts and sciences he was himself, despite his distraction with the affairs of state and his fierce pursuit of sensual pleasure, a philosopher and scholar of merit. He was an accomplished linguist and a profound student of the sciences of medicine and mathematics. With the exception of Albertus Magnus, no man in thirteenth century Europe was a greater authority on, or promoter of, the science of Natural History.

Of art in all its forms he was not only a patron but a proficient exponent. As a poet Frederick had few peers and the excellence of his verses in Italian won the unstinted praise of no less an authority than Dante, who called him the father of Italian poetry. He was a talented musician and composer, having few equals in this respect in the Italy of his day. He is said to have been a competent painter and architect and, although the evidence for this assertion is not so well founded, the taste and discrimination demonstrated in his art collections and extensive building prove that he was conversant with the theory if not the practice of these arts. Combined with such extraordinary skills, this highly endowed favorite of Nature possessed an acute legal mind. By an enlightened code of laws, his *Constitutiones* of 1231, he ranks with the great lawgivers of the West.

But unlike his cousin, Thomas, whom he so greatly resembled otherwise, Frederick was a completely selfish man. The great energy and gifts of mind that Thomas was to consecrate to the service of God and his fellow man, Frederick devoted entirely to himself. His court was the scandal of Europe. Frederick, himself, lived like a Moslem prince, harem and all, and openly repudiated Christianity.

Throughout his long reign, Frederick battled the Pope not only for temporal supremacy but spiritual supremacy as well. Old and broken, Honorius III was hardly a match for this devotee of Satan, but his successor Gregory IX, battled the perverse emperor to the death. Gregory won the battle, at least that is what the records say, but Frederick's fierce fight had not been in vain. So weakened was the Papacy that in the next battle of this great war for supremacy, that between Philip the Fair and Boniface VIII at the turn of the century, the Papacy lost its control — perhaps forever.

From the religious point of view it is correct to say, speaking generally, that in Thomas' time western Europe was still one fold and one shepherd. Eastern Europe, Asia, Asia Minor, and Africa had been almost entirely lost to the Church through attack from without and schism from within. Of these scourges the most dreadful, of course, had been that of Mohamet, which made its converts by fire and sword. In the time of Thomas, Islam, although dormant, still constituted a serious threat to the life of the Church.

Of the many eruptions from within, there are two which assumed the proportions of major heresies and which for a time appeared strong enough to topple the See of Peter — the Arian and the Albigensian. Both were Eastern in inspiration and ideology, and, though to the average Catholic today neither is more than a name, both were more virulent and more fiercely propagated than the Protestant Revolt of the sixteenth century.

At the time of Thomas' birth the second of these two, the Albigensian heresy, had reached its height. This fantastic error, which held that there were two gods — one good, one bad — had its origin in the early part of the twelfth century. For about a century the Church left it almost undisturbed, opposing it by only halfhearted measures. By the time of Innocent III, who was the immediate predecessor of Thomas' godfather, Honorius, on the papal throne, it had spread from the Danube to the Pyrenees and from Rome to England. It was strongest and most widespread in southern France, where lay the City of Albi, its principal stronghold. Innocent III declared that the Albigenses were more violent than the Saracens and that their teaching was more opposed to Christianity than the Koran. He recognized that, unless he were to stand idly by and watch this creeping death slowly strangle Mother Church, rigorous measures must be taken. Innocent opposed the virus by every means within his power including armed forces, but the best weapon for his hand was fashioned for him by God who, in this crisis, raised up St.

Dominic and his preaching brothers to attack the heretics on intellectual and ascetical grounds, battle fields beyond the reach of Innocent's soldiery. By the time of Thomas' birth, this gigantic struggle was in full swing. It was to continue almost until his death.

This, then, was the age in which Theodora's son lived his tremendous life. It was not a peaceful age and Thomas was not a peaceful man. The tiny babe at Rocca Sicca was destined to be a fighter — perhaps the greatest of his time, a cool and unruffled but scientific and deadly warrior. In him the Church was to find her greatest champion not only against the heresies but against the princes. Because of him it would require a more malicious man to be a Philip the Fair than a Barbarossa, and a Luther must needs use more energy than an Arius if he were effectively to close his ears to the voice of Truth.

Chapter 3

The Young Count's Schooldays

THE Church very nearly lost its champion while he was still an infant. During a violent storm on the night of June 1, 1231, lightning forked through the window of the nursery at Rocca Sicca and killed Theodora's youngest daughter. Thomas, lying at her side, slept peacefully on.

This is the only incident related of his childhood that bears the stamp of palpable truth. The other stories told by the early writers may or may not be true but they have too much of the edifying wonderful about them to be lightly believed. Ancient biographers were too prone to sprinkle miracles and wonderful happenings through their accounts of the infancy and childhood of a great man, especially if the great man happened to be a saint. However, the stories connected with the infancy of Thomas are not too incredible.

Thomas, according to one of these legends, was one day brought by his mother and nurse to the baths at Naples. As the two women were preparing to bathe the child, they noticed a small parchment roll in his hand. His nurse tried to take it from him but he held fast to his treasure and resisted her efforts with much yowling. His mother at last opened his hand and lo! the parchment contained but two words — *Ave Maria*. Theodora instantly returned her pious child's treasure to him and the infant seized it eagerly and swallowed it in imitation, say the early biographers, of Ezechiel the prophet.

Another tale from his babyhood relates a less pious but

equally edifying incident. One day, before he could walk alone, Thomas happened to find open the chest in which the family papers were kept. These papers were piled into the box in a haphazard fashion. Thomas, the chroniclers tell us, took them all out and arranged them in an orderly and systematic fashion before returning them to their place.

Count Landulf, who possessed in his two eldest sons insurance that the family name and prestige would be suitably continued, determined to give his third son to the Church. So at the age of seven, Thomas was sent to the neighboring Abbey of Monte Cassino to prepare himself for the priesthood in order that he might eventually become lord abbot of the famous old monastery, a post then held by his uncle Sinebald.

To the modern American mind this packing off of a son to the monastery may seem cruelty of an extreme sort. Why it should be cruel to dedicate a son to God in a monastery has never been sufficiently explained. Americans would not consider Landulf a heartless father because he dedicated two of his sons to the army. Nor would he be considered harsh had he prepared them for law or medicine or any other profession. But, to send a young, innocent, and ignorant boy to the monastery with the intention of making him a monk! This is one illustration of the dire results of medieval superstition! Today no one thinks of castigating a man, because he deliberately sets out to train his son to be a big-league pitcher. There are no cries of cruelty filling the air because many men have trained their sons to be football players. Why, then, should one be horrified because Count Landulf chose to train his boy for the monastery? Surely the profession the Count chose for his son was as respectable as those chosen by some Americans for theirs. If the profession suited Thomas he could choose it; if he disliked it, he could reject it. As a matter of fact the Count would not have been at all displeased if he had rejected it, because a house as prominent as his could easily use three sons to advantage. In dedicating Thomas to the service of God the Count was doing his best to be a good Catholic. To him the dedication represented a bit, not too much of course, but a bit of a sacrifice. The monastery of Monte Cassino to which the Aquinos entrusted their third son, was an abbey of the Benedictine monks. Monte Cassino had been founded by St. Benedict himself in 529, and within its walls great things had transpired during the centuries that had rolled over it. There both St. Benedict and his sister, St. Scholastica, had died. Saints without number had lived out their useful and placid lives there. Three times the abbey had been destroyed by God when earthquakes had overthrown it. Three times it had been razed by men — by the Lombards in 580, by the Saracens in 884 and again by the Normans in 1046.

The Aquino family had for long been connected with the abbey in various ways. The sons of the family had received whatever education they had at Monte Cassino. Several times the ancestors of Thomas had risked life and fortune in its defense. The abbey was, and still is, in the possession of the remarkable Order of St. Benedict, an institute which is today centuries older than any existing nation of Europe or the western hemisphere.

Greatly resembling the Church itself, Benedict's Order has witnessed the rise and fall of civilizations. It has seen and heard the comings and goings of false Christs and false prophets — and even false Benedictines. Benedict's sons have risen to great heights and have sunk to great depths in the course of their long history, yet the Order has always, by God's grace, been able to renew itself to such an extent, indeed, that in this twentieth century it offers to a man seeking God the strictest mode of life permitted by the Church. In the ebb and flow of the centuries the grand old Order has witnessed many successes and many vicissitudes. It has seen ages when it produced an Anselm, a Bernard, or a Bede; it has seen other periods when it produced little more than St. Bernard dogs and benedictine. The early thirteenth century is one of the low-water marks of Benedictine history. The Cistercians, a reform branch of the Order, were assigned by the Holy See to suppress the Albigensians. They failed miserably. Had the Benedictines been enjoying one of their many successful eras when they took in the child Thomas it is probable that he never would have left them. As it was they failed to measure up to his ideals. Thomas desired to be a priest and a monk, it is true, but he wanted it in an institute where there was less security and more apostolic and intellectual activity.

There is little known of Thomas' sojourn at Monte Cassino. It is recorded that he was a brilliant student and incessantly inquisitive about God. One of the first questions he asked his monk-master at the abbey was: "What is God?" He spent the rest of his life trying to find the answer. Thomas stayed at Monte Cassino for seven years. Before the end of that time the abbot, Uncle Sinebald, had passed to his eternal reward. By the time he was fourteen, Thomas had already learned all that the monks at Monte Cassino could teach him. Count Landulf arranged for his brilliant son to enter the University of Naples. Naples, a parvenu among European universities, was chosen because it was the only one that the Emperor Frederick would allow Neopolitan youths to attend.

So at the age of fourteen, the prodigy from Rocca Sicca fared forth from the sheltering confines of his monastery to the big, bad city of Naples. To say that Naples was both big and bad is no exaggeration. To the boy from the country it seemed monstrous in size and it was as bad, if not worse, than the other university cities of its day, where light life and lighter love seem to have been the chief preoccupation of most of the students.

But Theodora was not the mother to send her young son unprotected into this whirlpool. The Benedictines had at Naples two houses, San Severino and San Demetrio, both affiliated to Monte Cassino and it is probable that Thomas stayed at one or the other. There, in monastic solitude, the youthful genius continued his studies untouched by the whirling world, and the mind that had astounded the monks at Monte Cassino astounded no less the university professors. It was not long before his fame as a scholar spread throughout the university.

While Thomas was pursuing the higher learning at Naples, his rascally relative, Frederick II was doing his best to break the Pope's heart. After continued altercation and skirmishes with Pope Gregory IX, the pagan emperor determined to humble the pontiff. In 1238 he brought a huge army from Germany and laid waste northern Italy. So great was the slaughter that Frederick, with characteristic pride in carnage, boasted that the provinces were not large enough to bury the dead sacrificed to his vengeance. On Palm Sunday 1239, Gregory solemnly excommunicated the rebellious emperor and in retaliation Frederick redoubled his attack on the Church. Among the institutions pillaged was Monte Cassino where the treasures of the sanctuary were taken as booty and the monks were murdered without mercy. Having laid waste the entire northern country the infidel then marched his army on Rome. In 1240 he laid siege to the city but was unable to take it. So Frederick lifted the siege on the city but continued to ravage the Papal dominions. In 1241 Gregory weighed down by misfortune died of a broken heart.

In the meantime, Cousin Thomas used his genius in a different way. It was his ambition to consecrate his talents to God and the Church. How he could best do it was the problem that occupied his mind during a greater part of his stay at Naples. It became increasingly evident to him that he could never be satisfied as a Benedictine, so he continued his search. At last he discovered the Dominicans. Here he found the life that suited him. For a long time he practically lived in their chapel. Finally in 1242, when he was seventeen,

Thomas applied for admission to the Order. The prior of the convent refused to accept him. It seems likely that he did not wish to provoke the displeasure of Thomas' family and their powerful connections. Some writers have advanced the opinion that the candidate was too young, but this opinion has been based upon a faulty calculation of his age. It seems more probable that the Dominicans were not too eager to acquire this gem, which, while valuable, was too jealously guarded. Thomas was put off and advised to give serious thought to his vocation.

Chapter 4

You Can't Have My Son

THE Order of Preachers, of which Thomas aspired to become a member, had, so to speak, very low social rating at that time. Noblemen and those aspiring to ecclesiastical prestige certainly would not have chosen it as a stepping stone to high position. It drew its manpower from the four million rather than the four hundred, and its superiors were not, like the Benedictines of the day, listed in the society blue book *ex officio*. As a matter of fact Italian blue bloods turned up well-bred noses at the mention of the mendicant Order and a "good family" would have felt disgraced should a son so far forget his birth and breeding as to become a Dominican. The Sons of St. Dominic were in the social scale just a step above the Sons of St. Francis.

But, the Order of Preachers, notwithstanding its low social rating, was at this period in the first blush of its exuberant youth. It had been founded by Domingo de Guzmán, a Spanish priest of noble blood, incidentally, for the express purpose of combating the Albigensian heresy. On Dec. 22, 1216, the institute had received the approbation of the Holy See, principally because Thomas' godfather, Pope Honorius III had his back against the wall. The Pope was forced to recognize the new Order because the Albigensians had him at his wit's end. The Church had used every resource at her command to defeat the heretics and had failed. The fiery Guzmán promised the Pope that he could succeed.

He kept his promise. With the uncompromising zeal, un-flinching courage and irresistible magnetism of a saint, Guzmán, or St. Dominic, as he is called throughout the world today, struck the dragon its death blow. It did not die immediately and the Dominicans did not kill it unaided, but historians are agreed that it never recovered its pristine vigor after the fury of Guzmán's first fierce charge.

From his own battles with the sophistical heretics and from his observations of the inadequacy of the poorly trained Catholic clergy in refuting philosophical and theological error, St. Dominic determined that the men of his institute should receive the best intellectual training available, so he sent his first disciples to the university cities to sit at the feet of the great teachers of the time.

St. Dominic's successor, Jordan of Saxony, followed closely the ideals of the founder and lost little time erecting a convent of his Order at the new University of Naples. The Domini-cans arrived there a few years before St. Thomas. The Order of Preachers, as has been pointed out, was still very young, still very holy and very zealous. Its great founder had been dead about twenty years when the Order was established at Naples and the greatness of his spirit, the fire of his eloquence, the inspiration of his example still lived among them. The Dominicans soon drew the attention of the city and the university to themselves by their learning in the rostrum and their eloquence in the pulpit.

The prior of the Dominican convent at Naples was the learned Thomas Agni di Lentino, who afterward became Patriarch of Jerusalem, and one of the men who lived there was the celebrated preacher, John of St. Julian. Thomas Aquinas, casting about for a vocation in life, was greatly impressed by the combination of holiness and learning, typical of the Dominican spirit and exemplified by the Dominican friars at Naples. He decided to be a Dominican.

When the Prior recommended that he spend a year or

two in serious thinking and prayer before definitely making up his mind, the methodical Thomas did what he was told without question. At the expiration of the period, he applied once more for admission. In the meantime one great obstacle to his vocation had been removed from his path when God called Count Landulf to Himself. Count Landulf had been informed of his son's intention to become a mendicant friar and had been considerably annoyed at it. He did everything in his power to oppose the step. He threatened the friars, but the friars, we are told, refused to be intimidated. He pleaded with his son, but Thomas' mind was made up. And although we are assured that the Dominicans would have admitted Thomas into the Order even had the Count lived, the fact that they so long postponed his entrance certainly leaves this claim open to suspicion. It is possible, of course, that Landulf changed his mind. Perhaps, because he was a practical man, he came to the conclusion that since ordinary methods of persuasion had failed there would be little use in appealing to the extraordinary. Perhaps, too, because his strong life was almost over, the approach of the eternal years gave him a little different light in which to view things. At any rate, he is supposed to have given his reluctant consent. However, Landulf died in 1243, a year before Thomas received the habit of the Dominican Order.

When the news got abroad that the son of Count Landulf of Aquino, close blood relative of Frederick II and prominent at the university for his intellectual attainments, was to be received publicly into the mendicant Order of Preachers, the town as well as the gowns were agog. On the day of his reception, standing room in the church was at a premium. Everybody who was anybody made it a point to attend and much whispering took place on the campus concerning the sharpness of these friar fellows in landing so large a fish. At the appointed time, the largely built, handsome young squire from Rocca Sicca advanced to the altar between two

rows of friars and, in the simple ceremony characteristic of
the Order, received the habit of St. Dominic and became a
Dominican novice.

When Theodora heard the news of her son's self-imposed
degradation she was incensed. She saw all her castles in the
air falling into ruins about her. She had no objection to
her son becoming a priest — in fact, she had hoped and
prayed that God would grant her this favor. But in her
dreams Thomas had been more than a mere priest — he had
been lord abbot or Pope. And now he upon whom the whole
structure of her dream world rested had, like an impatient
Atlas, shaken his shoulders and sent it crashing. Furthermore,
he had not been content to relinquish the abbacy by becoming
a secular priest but he had chosen to become a mendicant
friar who begged his daily bread from door to door, dragging
the proud Aquino name with him as he went.

Theodora resolved that no son of hers would do such
a thing. He might be a starry-eyed dreamer who didn't know
what was best for him, but she was a woman of the world.
She was practical and clear-headed. She knew that great and
lofty ideals are all right in their place but power and position
are what count in this world. She determined to save her
son from himself by any means, fair or foul. She would
plead with him. Perhaps the sight of his grief-stricken mother
on her knees before him would melt his heart. Failing in
that, she would bring pressure upon the Holy See. If these
devices failed, other means she was convinced would be
found. When Thomas grew older he would thank her.

Thomas, suspecting that the countess would not relinquish
him without a battle, begged his superiors to send him out
of the kingdom as soon as he was received. The superiors
complied with his request and before the countess reached
Naples her son was on the road to Rome. The frustrated
mother set out posthaste to the eternal city. Arriving there
she went to the Dominican convent of Santa Sabina and

demanded to see her son. The brother porter informed the noble lady that Brother Thomas refused to interview her.

Fearing the length to which Theodora's passion might lead her and seeing that in Rome their prize novice was not beyond the reach of her long arm the authorities of the Order decided to send Brother Thomas far away, out of Italy entirely, to distant Cologne. It had been a mistake to bring Thomas to Rome in the first place. The Dominican superiors should have known that a woman of such high birth and position was capable of making trouble in any part of Italy. When Thomas refused to see his mother on her arrival at Santa Sabina all the forces of her strong, passionate nature where concentrated in anger. She denounced the Dominicans to the Pope himself. Not content with that she began to stir up the wrath of the powerful Roman nobility who were always capable, when roused, of making things uncomfortable even for the Pope. The Dominicans dodged the impending storm by spiriting Thomas out of the city.

When Theodora learned that she had been once more foiled by the crafty friars she took the step that she had hoped to avoid. She determined to have Thomas captured and brought back to Rocca Sicca by force. There she would hold him against the Papal armies if necessary. In Theodora's veins, it seems, there was more than a trickle of robber-baron blood. The countess dispatched a courier to her two elder sons, Landulf and Reynaldo, who were with Frederick's army near Acqua-Pendente, and informed them of her pleasure in regard to Thomas. The two officers of the imperial armies had the roads to France put under surveillance and the un-suspecting friars walked like rabbits into the soldiers' snare.

Thomas was seized and sent back to Rocca Sicca under a strong guard. There he was dragged, like an unruly child, before his mother. Theodora's outraged love and hurt pride left little tenderness in her feelings toward her bad boy. Thomas was lectured by the countess upon his duties to his house. Its fortunes were failing, she told him. If he would be sensible and accept the positions in the Church to which his birth entitled him, these fortunes could be retrieved. Why must he run off with this pack of beggars? Would not her dear son change his mind for the love of his mother and the honor of his house? To all the mother's pleadings her son remained adamant. Though his nature rebelled at the stand he was taking and though his heart was torn by the sight of his mother's tears, he remained faithful to his vocation and calmly rejected her pleas. Since tears availed her nothing, Theodora fell back to her final defense. She informed Thomas that since he persisted in being stubborn, he would be detained at the castle as a prisoner until he saw the light. So into a wing of the castle, called the Tower of San Giovanni, and placed under a heavy guard, went the third son of Count Landulf of Aquino, Lord of Belcastro and Loretto.

Chapter 5

One Year in Jail

THOMAS' imprisonment, while it was more than the mere detention of an unruly son, was not as harsh as was the custom in those days. He was not chained and the room in which he was confined was no dark dungeon but a fairly comfortable tower chamber with a fireplace and windows. The treatment accorded him was that ordinarily given to a respected political hostage or a noble prisoner of war. The greatest punishment he had to endure was separation from his brethren and deprivation of his books.

He was allowed social intercourse only with the members of his family, which meant his two sisters, for his brothers were in the field with the imperial armies and his mother, after her unsuccessful attempt to change his mind, troubled him no more. The proud countess found her defeat a bitter dose to swallow. So the two sisters, Theodora and Marietta, were the only human beings Thomas was allowed to see. They took turns serving his meals and, since they were in perfect accord with the rest of the family upon the vocation of their recalcitrant brother, poor Thomas was subjected several times daily to that form of persistent persuasion that the female of the species has developed to a high art — nagging.

But for once, at least, women had met a man who could match their exhausting persistence by his own inexhaustible patience. Thomas would listen again and again to their reiterated arguments subtly interlarded with those blandishments and flattery that women, almost intuitively, know how to use so skillfully. The flattery fell on deaf ears but the oft-answered arguments Thomas would continue to answer, each time approaching the objection from a different angle and each time presenting his own justification in a new light. The result was that the would-be proselytizers were converted and Thomas gained two friends in the camp of the enemy. So well did Thomas present his case that the two missionaries themselves received new starts in life. Marietta became a nun. Theodora, although she remained in the world, led an exemplary life and remained devoted to Thomas until her death.

Through the agency of his converts, Thomas was able to get in touch with his Dominican brethren in Naples and from them he received what he most wanted — books. His sisters smuggled into his cell copies of the *Bible,* the *Sentences of Peter Lombard,* and some of the works of Aristotle. He also received visits from Father John of St. Julian, famous Dominican preacher of the time, who brought him not only spiritual consolation but badly needed clothes. The Dominican habit which Thomas wore when arrested was much the worse for wear, for the countess had sworn that until her son would consent to don either the Benedictine habit or the apparel of a layman, no more clothes would be given him.

How long Thomas was left with this added peace we do not know but it is certain that after a time the imperial armies returned to the vicinity of Rocca Sicca, bringing with them, of course, the two elder sons of the family. Then Thomas' peace was rudely disturbed. The brothers, arriving unexpectedly at the castle one day, discovered the Dominican, John of St. Julian, on the premises and had him immediately jailed. Going up to Thomas' cell, they found their stubborn brother all dressed up in a new habit.

They concluded that the sisters had betrayed their trust and they immediately deprived them of their charge. The brothers themselves then took over the task of breaking Thomas' spirit. They invited some of their army friends to visit them and entertained them in Thomas' cell, singing their lewd army songs and telling their lascivious soldier stories. But Thomas remained unmoved by their drunken parties and army-camp sports. He withdrew farther into himself and if anyone was annoyed it was the revellers who were trying so hard to have a good time in spite of this imperturbable friar who sat in the midst of them, removed and remote, a specter at the feast.

Since all their other resources had failed to budge their serene brother, the soldiers considered the time had come to let the emergency ace slip out of their sleeve. It was necessary that his serenity be shaken, his imperturbability disturbed, his strength of will broken. Heretofore, their assaults upon their brother's iron will had been repelled with ridiculous ease. The brothers were convinced that the secret of his strength lay in his purity. He must be robbed of that tremendous weapon if they were to have their way. No one more keenly appreciates the power of purity than do the impure. Throughout the course of history, scoundrels have always used sexual pleasure as the best instrument to sap spiritual strength. From the Roman emperors down to the French and Spanish Masons of the last century and the Communists of our own day this has been the chief weapon in the arsenal of anti-Christians in their attack upon Christian youth. So the brothers of Thomas reasoned that their prisoner must be robbed of his mysterious treasure. Thomas must be seduced!

The matter was arranged with a beautiful young Neapolitan woman who, for a consideration, agreed to undertake the task. Nothing whatever is known for certain about the girl except that she was young and beautiful. She flits across the pages of history like a gaudy humming bird, for certainly her transit across the life of Thomas was swift enough — as swift as her flight from his cell. She was probably not a common woman in the usual sense of that word; it is more likely that she was a high class courtesan, who catered to the nobility. Thomas' biographers have very modestly drawn the veil over the whole affair. They relate only that the saint as soon as he learned her business in his chamber acted with surprising speed. Rushing to the fireplace, he seized a burning brand and flourishing it at the dumbfounded girl he chased her from the room, burning a cross into the door through which she made her hasty exit — an exit as lacking in dignity as her womanhood.

According to the earliest biographies, the saint was then girded with a cord by angels from heaven on the following night as he slept. This act of the heavenly messengers was to signify to Thomas that he was to be freed, for the rest of his life, from temptations of the flesh. Although this anticlimax to the story of the temptation of Thomas has all the earmarks of the medieval love for the miraculous, the fact remains that the antiquity of the tale lends it credibility. St. Thomas, upon his death, is supposed to have given a cord to his faithful friend and confessor, Reginald of Piperno. Reginald, in turn, gave it to Philip the Bold of France, a cousin of St. Thomas, and Philip gave it to the Dominican Master General, John of Vercelli. John transferred the relic to the Dominican convent at Vercelli where it remained until the Napoleonic Wars, when it was carried off by the last prior of that house, Father Benedict Caramelli, for safe keeping. In 1821 it was brought to the Dominican priory at Piedmont where it has remained ever since. There are few relics that have a more authentic history. So highly do the Dominicans value the relic that they have refused to part with it even against the plea of the Holy Father himself. The incident of the girding of Thomas inspired the founding of the confraternity known as *The Angelic Warfare,* a society, under the patronage of the Order of Preachers designed to aid Catholic youth to preserve its chastity.

How far Thomas' brothers would have gone in their persecution is hard to say because after the incident of the attempted seduction they were not given much opportunity. The Pope had received word of Thomas' imprisonment and ruffianly treatment and the Vicar of Christ had risen in righteous wrath at such treatment being meted out to an ecclesiastic. Not even to be awed by the power of the Aquinos, the successor of Peter, who unflinchingly faced emperors, demanded the young Dominican's release. In the Pope's demand lurked the threat of excommunication and the relatives of Thomas, while willing to flout the Pope and pull his beard to a degree, feared the apostolic anathema.

Yet their pride would not allow them to admit they were forced to free the prisoner. The family's face must be saved at all events. So Thomas was allowed to escape. Aided by his sisters he was let down, like St. Paul of old, from the tower in a basket into the arms of his Dominican brethren waiting below. That was some time in the late summer of 1245 after he had been in prison for over a year. The Dominicans set out for their convent at Naples, rejoicing that the sheep that was lost had been found.

Thomas was free from prison and once more back with his Dominican brethren at Naples but his mother had not yet given up the fight. She appealed to the Holy See to annul her son's vows, telling the Pope that the wily Dominicans had tricked him into taking them. Innocent IV summoned Thomas before him to hear his side of the case. Thomas, appearing before the papal court to plead his own case, repudiated his mother's statement. He informed the head of the Church that his entering the Order of Preachers had been of his own volition and he had no intention of abandoning his vocation. He said he had no reproach for his mother and brothers for the treatment they had meted out to him, because they were naturally disappointed in the course he had elected. He was deeply sorry, he stated, that his conscience would not allow him to act as they desired him to act.

The Pope then offered to make Thomas Abbot of Monte Cassino, allowing him at the same time to retain his membership in the Dominican Order and wear the Dominican habit. But Thomas resolutely declined. He wanted no dignity and honors, he averred; his only desire was to remain a simple friar and be allowed to pursue his vocation in peace. The Pope returned judgment in his favor. *Roma locuta est; causa finita.* This ended Thomas' troubles with his family. They gave up the fight for the nonce and allowed him to go his way.

Chapter 6

Thomas at Paris

SOON after the Pope pronounced judgment in favor of Thomas, the Master General of the Order, John of Wildeshausen, better known as John the German, assigned the young Neapolitan to the Dominican convent of St. James in Paris to pursue his studies in theology at the University of Paris, then the leading university of the Christian world. Thomas in the company of the Dominican Master General arrived at the French capital, where his cousin, St. Louis, ruled as king, in the Autumn of 1245. It was then he met for the first time the man who, more than any other, was to form the mind of the greatest thinker of the Christian world. This man was Albert of Suabia, universally known in the history of thought as Albert the Great.

At the time when Thomas came to Paris, Albert was a professor in the Order's studium in that city. He was not only the greatest scholar of his Order but the greatest of his time and holds first rank among the philosophers of all time. Albert, like his new disciple, was of noble birth and had been a student at the University of Padua when, in 1228, he heard Jordan of Saxony, the second Master General of the Dominicans, preach a sermon which resulted in Albert's joining the Order. By 1245 the reputation of his great learning was beginning to spread. In that year Albert received his doctorate at the University of Paris, although he had been teaching at the Dominican convent for a decade and was recognized as the outstanding professor of the city. It was to Albert that the two Spanish princes, the sons of Ferdinand III of Castile who were studying at the university, went for direction. That they should have selected him from among the hundreds of professors in the city seems to indicate a certain prominence — and this was as early as 1235.

Before Albert left Paris in 1248 he had become not only a famous but a legendary figure. He was a profound and constant student of the natural sciences and his researches in this direction, considered dangerous and profane by many thinkers of the day, had led to dark stories being circulated about him. These stories were to grow, as Albert's experiments continued, until it would be commonly believed that he had sold his soul to the devil.

It is not upon the great Suabian's researches in natural science that his most lasting claim to fame must rest but upon his work in bringing Aristotle out of the East, a prodigious labor that consumed a lifetime. The text of Aristotle had been corrupted by the Jews and the Arabians and before the time of Albert the Stagirite had been the most formidable intellectual enemy the Church had yet faced. Albert started his study of the great Greek with an open mind and made every attempt to obtain an authentic and uncorrupted text. His lectures on the logic, ethics, and physics of Aristotle at Paris aroused such enthusiasm that no building in the city was large enough to accommodate the throng that crowded to hear them.

In spite of the prodigious amount of work that Albert accomplished, he probably would have done much more had not the burdens of office been thrust upon him. In 1254 he was elected provincial of the German Dominicans and he had hardly been released from that office when he was appointed to another, for on January 9, 1260, he was made Bishop of Ratisbon. But we will hear more of Albert as this sketch progresses. This brief outline of his life is here given because that life is so closely interwoven with the life of Thomas that it is necessary to know Albert to have a complete knowledge of Aquinas.

Little is known of Thomas' student life in Paris. In fact so little has come down to us from that period that many biographers of Thomas assume that he stopped off there only for a rest before continuing his journey to Cologne. However, it is well established from Mandonnet's chronology of the saint's life that he stayed there three years and did not leave the French capital until he went with Albert to the newly erected house of studies in Cologne in 1248.

It is rather surprising that this period of his life should be so obscure. What happened to the scholastic brilliance that attracted the notice of Naples? This question could be easily answered by saying that the young friar's intellectual light shone only in his own convent and that the city at large did not have the opportunity to gape in wonderment at it. That would be a fine and satisfying answer were it not for the fact that it was about this time that he received the soubriquet, "the dumb ox." One reason that can be given for Thomas' apparent intellectual eclipse is that he retired into himself. He began to think deeply upon the matter he studied and as he thought and reflected he saw the difficulties more thoroughly and appreciated the many sides, presented by seemingly simple problems, more completely. The brilliance that caused him to be acclaimed at Naples, the quick mind, the marvelous memory, these he still retained but greater maturity of intellect found a new use for these dazzling qualities. In Naples they had been used as a mirror, reflecting the sun of truth with stupefying luster; in Paris they were used as a burning glass, concentrating the rays into a minute point. The intellectual life of "the angel of the schools" had begun in earnest.

In Paris, the bustling "city of philosophers," still more bustling by the addition of 20,000 university students to its native population of 100,000, Brother Thomas found the

cloistered peace and quiet necessary for serious study. How
this was possible appears to be something of a miracle. It was
not that the Dominican convent of St. James was situated
in a semirustic site on the outskirts of the city. On the
contrary, the convent stood in the crowded island in the Seine
in the very heart of the university. Nor was the peace of the
convent due to the fact that its doors were barred to seculars,
for secular students swarmed through its portals to attend
the lectures given by Albert and other famous Dominican
masters. Its peace was due to the strict religious discipline
which divided the working day into rigid compartments, each
section dedicated to a certain exercise. Thus at the end of the
lecture period the business of the secular students at the
convent was finished for the day. The rest of the day was
dedicated by the friars to prayer and study.

The Convent of St. James at Paris was one of the oldest
houses of the young Order. When St. Dominic dispersed
his sons, he dispatched seven of them to Paris. Arriving there
the friars rented a house in the heart of the city not far from
the bishop's palace. Their activity in Paris so impressed the
king's physician, John of St. Alban, that he transferred to
them the buildings which he had built at the university for
the Benedictines to serve as a house of hospitality for pilgrims.
This *hospitium* had been dedicated to St. James of Com-
postella. The Dominicans retained him as patron for their
convent. In 1221 at the request of Pope Honorius the University of Paris transferred the title of the land to the preaching friars. In return for the gift the Dominicans promised to
celebrate a Solemn Mass for all living members of the
university each year on the eighth of December and a Solemn
Requiem Mass for all departed members annually on
February third. The masters of the University enjoyed a
share in the suffrages and spiritual works of the Order.
If a member of the theological faculty died he could, if he
so wished, be buried in the chapter-room of the convent;

a member of any other faculty might claim the right to be buried in the cloister.

The first Convent of St. James was in poor repair when the sons of Dominic first went to live there. This condition was improved by St. Louis, King of France, who built them a new convent. The religious and intellectual life of the convent had been early stimulated by St. Dominic himself, who lived there for a time. At the time when Thomas studied there the benign shadow of the great Spaniard still hung over its cloisters. In this atmosphere of holiness and intellectuality St. Thomas lived for three years and grew in wisdom and in grace.

Chapter 7

The Dumb Ox Bellows

IN the summer of 1248 Thomas went with Albert to
Cologne, the former to study at the recently opened
Dominican University; the latter to become its regent of
studies or president. The Dominicans were not newcomers
to the German metropolis. They had first established themselves there in 1221, when Blessed Jordan of Saxony and
Henry of Cologne, two of St. Dominic's most faithful
students in the science of the saints, opened a house near
the Cathedral with a chapel dedicated to St. Mary Magdalen
attached.

The Dominicans soon attracted the attention of the whole
city. So holy and abstemious were they that the people could
hardly believe that they were priests. The secular clergy of
Cologne, as a class, could hardly be called apostolic. They
were a bluff, hearty lot addicted to the pleasures of the flesh
both licit and illicit. In a sermon preached in the city, St.
Albert the Great castigated them unmercifully. He compared
the clergy of Cologne to the barren woman of the Gospels
who had married seven brothers one after another. Albert
pointed out that while the woman was clever enough to get
herself seven men as husbands she was unable to produce
offspring by any of them. Like unto her, said Albert, was
the Cologne clergy. They were smart enough to get themselves good livings but they produced no fruit therefrom.

The clergy, of course, could not appreciate such uncivil
conduct upon the part of the Dominicans. Neither did they

33

relish the way the people of the city flocked to the chapel
of St. Mary Magdalen, overcrowding it for every public
service. Anything but music to their ears was the praise of
the new preachers to be heard in all quarters. They begged
Archbishop Englebert to expel the disturbers. Englebert
replied that as long as the only charge to be made against
the friars was the good they did he would not disturb them.
In vain did the priests endeavor to persuade the Archbishop
that these friars, with their strange clothing and shaven
heads, were the men referred to by St. Hildegard and who
she had foretold would bring the city to its ruin. The
Dominicans remained.

At the convent in Cologne St. Thomas continued the
studies he had pursued in Paris. He still failed to show the
brilliance which at Naples had characterized him as a
student. If anything Thomas, at Cologne, retired more within
himself; so much so indeed that he gave his fellow students
the impression of immense and supine stupidity. The dumb
ox of Sicily became the butt of his classmates' jokes. It would
seem that in hours when the younger friars were not
occupied with prayer or study the stupid Italian was always
good for a laugh. Ridicule is not an unknown thing in
convents and there it is possibly a more stinging thing than
in the world, for wits sharpened by philosophic study are
capable of devising, at times, sharper practical jokes, though
comparatively less cruel, than those thought up by men in
the world. Also, because of restricted opportunities for
recreation there is the very human tendency to devise one's
own humor and ever since man has lived on earth practical
joking has been a basic form of this art.

Everything points to the fact that at this period of his life
his fellow students considered Thomas a lout. The authentic
stories concerning him preserved for posterity are not good
examples of convent humor. They are extremely childish and
somewhat crude. It is a certainty that many other and better

anecdotes were suppressed because they might disedify the reader. However, the few that have come down to us definitely show one side of the saint's character. He evidently played well the part of dim-wit which had been assigned him. He allowed himself to be the perennial dupe, the butt of all humor. He kept his tongue in his cheek and could always be easily victimized by the wits of the convent.

The question that naturally enters the reader's mind is: why should he have made himself such a gull? The answer seems to be fairly obvious. St. Philip Neri made himself the laughing stock of his community, did the most outrageous things so people would consider him a fool. Other saints have proceeded to fantastic lengths for the same object.

Thomas had made up his mind to be a saint, and pride, as he himself was to show so well in the writings of his later life, is the most obstinate obstacle to sanctity, for St. Augustine well says that while the other vices are responsible for the evil in bad actions the vice of pride is capable of making even a good action bad. There is more truth than humor in the story of the man who was humble and proud of that fact. Thomas came from a family which never possessed humility as a characteristic virtue. Practically every member of his family who has come to the notice of history was monstrously proud. Pride was the chief defect of the house. Thomas recognized that if he were to succeed in becoming a saint his efforts to combat pride must be extraordinary. His intellectual success at Naples, where he bested the university professors, seems to indicate that up to that time his progress in overcoming the family failing had not been too pronounced. His stubborn opposition to his mother's wishes, a combat that shook Italy, could have been as easily inspired by the vice of pride as by the virtue of perseverence. There is no certain indication up to the time that Thomas entered the Order of Preachers that he had succeeded in overcoming his weakness. This explanation is offered as the reason why the man who possessed one of the great minds of all time should have been considered the class fool by his fellows.

One of the stories from this period demonstrates how well Thomas succeeded in his self-imposed task. One day as he was studying in his cell he heard the voice of one of the brethren calling his name and insisting that he come to the window and witness a marvelous sight — that of an ox flying. Thomas, the ever willing dupe, apparently believing the story, came to the window and scanned the heavens. Of course his action provoked great hilarity from the joker and his confederates. Thomas searched for the reported wonder to the accompaniment of loud guffaws. When questioned as to why even he could be taken in by such a ridiculous tale Thomas quietly answered that he'd rather believe it possible for an ox to fly than that a friar could lie.

However, the brethren were not always unkind to their weak-minded fellow. Sometimes they pitied his stupidity and endeavored to aid him in his struggles to acquire a smattering of learning. An anecdote is told of one such attempt. A fellow student was instructing Thomas in theology and probably hoping that he could pound at least a few fundamentals into the thick skull of the wide-eyed, massive Italian. The self-appointed professor was getting on very well with the lesson until he came to a rather difficult passage. He hemmed and hawed trying to explain something he did not himself understand. Finally away beyond his depth with his entire supply of self-inflation exhausted, he was about to drown in his own meaningless verbiage. Thomas, ever the champion of truth, was forced to discard his mask. Gently taking the book from the floundering pedagogue, Aquinas explained the difficulty with great clearness and precision to his astounded instructor. The young friar, astonished at the brilliance of the Italian count, begged him to be his tutor for the future. Thomas at first refused but finally consented on the stipulation that the matter be kept a complete secret.

It seems that St. Albert, who had taught Thomas for three years at Paris, was unaware of the student's brilliance. Albert did not discover the fact until some time after the above incident and then quite by accident. During the course of a series of lectures which Albert was giving on the tract *De Divinis Nominibus* of Dionysius, a folio of notes that Thomas had made on the lectures fell into his hands. Albert was able to read Thomas' wretched scribbling well enough to see that the commentary could have been produced by no second-rate mind. He could hardly believe that the dolt of the school was capable of such incisive thinking, so he determined to settle the matter at once. He commanded Thomas to prepare for a public defense of the thesis and when the day of the disputation arrived, Albert himself assumed the role of objector.

In the clash of the two greatest intellects then existing in the world, Thomas emerged the victor. After Thomas had replied with irrefutable logic to his professor's fourth subtle objection, crushing his opponent with a stunning distinction, Albert addressed him. "You do not speak," he said, "as one on the defensive but as a master expounding the truth." In St. Thomas' answer is contained the keynote of his whole teaching life. "I can see no other way," he replied, "of answering the objections." Thomas was to demonstrate that a good offensive was the best defense of truth and that many objections would be still-born if the defender's exposition was clear and incisive. It was at this juncture that Albert turning to the crowded lecture hall prophesied, "You call this man a dumb ox but I tell you that the time will come when the bellowing of his doctrine will be so loud that it will be heard to the ends of the earth." After this unveiling, involuntary though it was, Albert compelled Thomas to teach the course. The manuscript copy of the notes the Angelic Doctor made for this course are still extant.

Chapter 8

The Return to Paris

HAVING discovered the brilliance of his disciple, Albert resolved not to allow that brilliance to be lost to the world no matter what ideas Thomas might have on that subject. Being regent of studies for the convent, he possessed considerable authority and influence. He now used both for the purpose of bringing the great powers of Aquinas to their full development. He arranged to have the Italian's cell next to his own. He encouraged Thomas to share in his own experiments and he put the extensive notes of his own discoveries at the student's disposal. He selected the young man as his companion at recreation; they took their walks together. In short, Albert set out with typical Teutonic thoroughness to develop Thomas. He realized that he had been entrusted with a mind superior to his own. Instead of being moved by envy, Albert was delighted. The pupil was destined to outshine the master — Albert must have known this. But to him that meant nothing. He would find his greatest glory in the fact that he had a share in the shaping of Aquinas. This was the beginning of the friendship between St. Albert the Great and Thomas, a friendship that ranks with the famous friendships of the ages. The two Gregory's, Francis and Dominic, John and Teresa — none were closer than Albert and Thomas. When Thomas came to write his tract on the *amor amicitiae* — the love of friendship — he could write as one having experimental knowledge. Next to the gifts of intellect and final perseverance, God gave the angel of the schools no finer gift than Albert.

Although the exact date cannot be ascertained, it seems that Thomas was ordained to the priesthood not long after he dazzled Albert and his fellow students in the public disputation which took place in the year 1250. For between this date and the time he left for Paris it is recorded that when Albert was away from Cologne on business, as he often was, Thomas not only mounted his rostrum but he likewise filled his master's pulpit. There is no need to speculate, as some have, on the feelings that filled the breast of the man from Rocca Sicca on that day of days when he was granted the divine power to recreate the Passion of our Blessed Lord; to cause to be present on the altar the almighty divinity and magnificent humanity of Jesus Christ. Anyone who has been even slightly scorched by what has been aptly termed the "frozen fire" of the great eucharistic hymns, already has some appreciation of the feelings of Aquinas on the day of his ordination. A better commentary upon the event could not be written. Let us leave that commentary as it stands and eschew vain and feeble speculation.

While Thomas was still at Cologne his family made one more attempt to reclaim him. In 1250 misfortune struck the proud family of Aquino. For in that year Frederick II went to his eternal reward and the office of Holy Roman Emperor fell to Conrad IV. On the throne of Peter sat Innocent IV, against whom Conrad, true to the tradition of the German emperors, immediately took up arms. This time, however, the Aquinos were on the right side. They espoused the cause of the Pope. Why this change of allegiance, is difficult to determine. Some say that the Aquinos abandoned Frederick when he was excommunicated by the Council of Lyons. Yet the fact remains that the family had adhered to their emperors and kinsmen through previous anathemas of the Holy See. Others claim that the family was reformed through the constant prayer of Thomas on their behalf. The old writers point out that Theodora died in the odor of sanctity. They tell us that after Thomas became a Dominican, she spent her life in prayer, penance, and the works of charity. "She macerated her body," says Frigerio, "with long fasting and frequent vigils, while she nourished her soul with the Divine food of prayer. So constant were her prayers and genuflections (in which she imitated St. James, the apostle) that the skin of her knees became hardened."

While this has all the earmarks of a pious and edifying story, it is certainly anything but unreasonable. We know that Thomas converted his two sisters and that Marietta became a Benedictine nun and Abbess of a monastery at Capua. It is an historical fact that Theodora, the younger sister, became the wife of the Count of Marisco and lived a life of virtue. It would be strange, indeed, if the mother remained obdurate in the face of all this good example. It is very likely that she became a holy woman as the early writers picture her.

And the bad brothers, Landulf, Count of Aquino, and Reynaldo, Count of Sora, who had gone to such unseemly lengths to break Thomas' spirit, they, too, did penance of the most violent kind. For when Conrad took up arms against the Pope, the Aquinos were the first to feel the weight of his wrath. Conrad captured the castle of Aquino and razed it to the ground, the town of Aquino was given to the torch and the sword, and the brothers were taken prisoners. Landulf was sent into exile where he died and Reynaldo, who, incidentally is supposed to have introduced the temptress to Thomas' chamber, was starved to death in prison.

But before calamity of such staggering proportions fell upon the family, while its fortune was in a badly damaged but still retrievable condition, the brothers once more appealed to Thomas to accept ecclesiastical dignity. The appeal was refused. Whatever may have been his motives the first time, whether stubborn Teutonic pride may have been mixed with high ideals and genuine humility, this second appeal was rejected by Thomas, the saint, through the firm conviction that his soul's salvation lay in fidelity to his vocation. Thomas' love of his family, which is demonstrated throughout his life, would not have permitted him to refuse to help them for any less grave reason.

It may seem unnatural and hardhearted to us that Thomas should refuse his help at this crisis. Possibly he would have helped even at the risk of his own salvation could he have seen any practical advantage to be derived by the change. But it was quite evident that ecclesiastical dignity would serve as no protection against Frederick or his savage sons. The revenues from an abbey or bishopric might bolster the family fortunes but to what end? More squandering. A family that had succeeded in dissipating the immense patrimony that had been the Aquinos' would surely make short work of the resources of a bishopric or abbey. This is the prospect that faced Thomas. Calm and clear eyed as always he could see no real advantage coming to his beloved family by a change of vocation. He remained a Dominican at Cologne, making giant strides in the sacred sciences and philosophy under the tutelage of Albert.

Albert was determined that nothing should stand in the way of his brilliant disciple's full development. By 1252 he decided that if Thomas were to continue his intellectual growth it was necessary that he matriculate at Paris for his bachelor's degree. This step required the approbation of the Master General of the Order and although John the German was favorable to Thomas he refused his permission, principally, it seems, because Thomas was too young. A bachelor at Paris was supposed to be at least thirty-five years of age and Thomas at this time was but twenty-seven. But Albert was determined that no such nonessential condition would be allowed to retard the growth of his student. He immediately set about surmounting the obstacle. Using all of his influence and enlisting the aid of the Dominican cardinal, Hugh of St. Cher, who was then at Cologne, he succeeded in changing the minds of both the General and the university authorities. In the summer of 1252 Thomas went to Paris. He started immediately to lecture, laying thereby the foundation stones of the monumental edifice of theological and philosophical writing which have preserved his name to the ages.

Chapter 9

Seculars Versus Regulars

THOMAS traveled from Cologne to Paris on foot as all
friars traveled in that day. On his way thither he stopped
to preach at the court of Margaret, Duchess of Brabant.
According to some biographers it was then that Thomas
promised to write a philosophical treatise on the government
of the Jews. This is most probably somebody's guess because
Thomas did not write his treatise *De Regime Judaeorum* for
fifteen or twenty years after this date. We may be sure that
if Thomas had promised such a treatise to the duchess, she
would not have had to wait that long. That was not the
way Thomas did things. It is much more probable that the
Duchess of Brabant was an old friend of the Aquino family
and that this visit Thomas paid to her in 1252 was not
his last.

Arriving at Paris, Thomas walked into an arena where
two opposing forces were girding for battle. During the
previous February the secular professors at the university had
publicly denounced the friars teaching there. No one
realized, on that day in late summer, when the huge man,
clad in the black and white habit of St. Dominic, trudged
the slight slope of Mount St. Genevieve toward the Dominican convent of St. James, that the champion of the friars had
arrived. There were brilliant men among the friars at Paris
anyone of a dozen of whom, one might suspect, would be
the knight to bring victory to the friars. No one who saw

the great, hulking form of the young count from Italy that day would have thought it would be he. No one suspected that without him things would have gone badly for the friars.

When Thomas left Cologne behind him he left behind his days of undisturbed peace. In coming to Paris he was entering the field of battle. There he would don the harness of war and remain in it until death. This is just one of the poignant features in his life — that he who so much loved peace and solitude should find himself always in the midst of strife. But he accepted his role as the champion of truth with the same equanimity that he accepted everything else in life. If he had to fight to defend truth then he would fight, and that was that. He fought magnificently. Never with rancor, never with anger but calmly, scientifically and, this above all, with surpassing charity. Faced with an adversary who was a mere dialectician, in the worse sense of that word, an adversary who cared nothing for truth but only for victory in debate, Thomas remained as kind and calm as though he were instructing the most earnest truth seeker. But we are getting somewhat ahead of our story. Let us return to Paris and the defense of the friars.

The animosity which the secular professors of Paris entertained for the regulars was of long standing. Like a hidden cancer which had been eating away at the breast of the secular faculty in secret for years, it finally erupted on the surface in February, 1252, with the public denunciation referred to. There is a tendency on the part of friar historians to attribute the whole strife to jealousy on the part of the seculars because of the success of the Dominican and Franciscan professors. These point out that the greatest professors of the age were friars. It cannot be denied that the success that attended the efforts of the great friar teachers provoked the jealousy of the secular professors, but the more important cause was more deeply rooted and fundamental than that. The friars were merely the immediate object of a hatred of Christianity itself. The University of Paris, long the greatest intellectual defender of Christianity, had become intellectually corrupt and morally bankrupt. For many years the virus of Arabian philosophy which had entered its body had been slowly creeping through the blood stream until it reached the heart, the theological faculty.

The intellectuals of Europe had long been fascinated by the philosophy of Aristotle and many were attracted not only from Paris but from every great university of Europe to the Arabian schools which were the centers of Aristotelian philosophy. The unfortunate side of the whole affair was that the Arabians did not teach the true Aristotle but Aristotle as adapted to fit the fantastic errors and unreal philosophy of the East; Aristotle as interpreted by such imaginative dreamers as Theophrastus and Philoponus; Aristotle as expounded by such architects of the never never land as Avincenna and Averöes. Yet Aristotle even so deformed with the shape of a hideous monster enchanted the minds of the European scholars.

The University of Paris gradually became the European center of these fairyland philosophies of the effete East. By the beginning of the thirteenth century its theological faculty had been partially corrupted by the noxious miasma and that corruption was spreading rapidly. Scores of teachers of this great center of Christian culture were publicly propagating doctrines which were in direct antithesis to Christianity. In the late twelfth century Almaric of Bena taught outrageous blasphemy based on the principle that human nature was identical with the divinity. In the early thirteenth David of Dinant, a popular instructor, taught that God is primary matter. Both were condemned, but rather tardily, by the Church. As a result of the teaching of these two men the natural philosophy of Aristotle was also banned by the Church.

Nevertheless, despite these proscriptions, the oriental Aristotle continued to gain favor at the university. When the

Dominicans first arrived there to obtain the intellectual training they needed to combat the eastern-born heresy of the
Albigensians they discovered to their chagrin and amazement
that it would be far easier to learn how to support these
errors than to be trained to combat them, for here the same
vicious doctrines which they had been fighting in southern
France had donned the cap and gown. To their horror they
found that here in the very brain of Christ's mystical body,
that Christianity was old-fashioned, its teachings a matter
of public scorn, and its practices openly derided. The threat
to the Church offered by this deranged mind cannot be
imagined, for priests were leaving the university imbued with
the doctrines that were in the very air and dispersing
throughout the Christian world to propagate them.

The friars would have no part of this teaching. Followers
of Christ in doctrine as in action they immediately set up a
counteroffensive. The student body at the university found
itself attracted to the friars as the people of southern France
had been and the masters saw their grip upon the students
slowly slipping. University students not only went to hear
the Dominicans but they stayed to become Dominicans themselves. Masters who had been disciples of the new learning
left their chairs to join the Order. The *Domini canes*, the
watchdogs of the Lord, were raising a din, a fearful din and
the masters determined that these dogs would be muzzled.

In addition to making themselves troublesome in matters
philosophical, the friars, both Dominican and Franciscan,
were working their way into university chairs. The Dominicans, in particular, incurred the ire of the secular faculty by
the underhanded way they achieved this end. In 1229 the
Dominicans already had one chair in theology at the university, which in the minds of their antagonists had been
obtained in a questionable fashion.

In that year an event occurred that gave the preachers the
opportunity to obtain another. In a Paris tavern a group of

university ruffians of the François Villion type engaged in
a bloody brawl with some of the town hoodlums. Now, these
brawls were common enough happenings, for the antagonism
that existed between town and gown erupted periodically.
However, this particular brawl had been exceptionally bloody
and the townsmen took a terrific beating, several being killed.
The university gangsters were arrested by the town police.
The whole university, even the respectable portion of it,
became exceedingly indignant. Such a move on the part
of the town was unheard of, a gross infringement upon
university privileges. It was understood that the university
would take care of its own hoodlums, an assignment which
it usually performed in a half-hearted manner. The university
howled its indignation to the Pope and to the King. But both,
being sick and tired of the roughneck student body, turned
deaf ears. Thereupon, the masters and the student body
went on strike. The greater part of them moved out of Paris
in a body determined to leave the town to its well-
deserved fate.

The Dominicans and Franciscans refused to strike. They
remained behind to teach those who had been impervious
to mob psychology. Since the theological faculty had joined
the exodus new professors were needed to fill the vacant
chairs. The Dominicans were offered a second chair in
theology and they accepted it. When the strike was over and
the professors and the student body returned the Dominicans
refused to relinquish their new chair much to the disgust
of the secular faculty.

Another thing that roused the ire and envy of the secular
faculty was the success with which the religious, specifically
the Dominicans and Franciscans, played both ends against
the middle. These obnoxious friars seemed to possess a genius
for making the best of both worlds — the spiritual and
material. They went about with shaven poll and meek
expression preaching primitive Christianity. They spent long

hours in prayer and meditation. They practiced the evan-
gelical counsels, living lives of exemplary asceticism. Yet they
never missed an opportunity to snap up rich benefactions,
which because of the hold that the holy friars were getting
on the people became increasingly rich and more numerous
with the passing years. Thus, in spite of the fact that the
friars remained individually poor they became collectively
wealthy by robbing, so reasoned the secular faculty, the university priests of what was rightfully theirs.

And, of course, jealousy of the success of the friars as
teachers added fuel to the fire of secular opposition. With
nothing to do but study when not praying, and far removed
from the harrowing cares and distracting pleasures of the
world, the friars soon became the outstanding teachers in
Paris. They were the great professors at the university. Albert,
Thomas, Bonaventure, John of St. Giles, Vincent of Beauvais,
Alexander of Hales, Hugh of St. Cher, Roland of Cremona,
John of Rochelle — these were but a few of the bright lights
that shone in the intellectual firmament of the thirteenth
century. As time passed their ability and popularity increased
so that finally no hall at the university could contain the
crowds that flocked to hear Albert who had to deliver his
lectures in the open air, as did Thomas and Bonaventure
following him. These causes of strife rankled in the breast of
the secular faculty and Doctor Time, the overrated physician,
did nothing to alleviate the pain.

The public denunciation of the regulars by the secular
faculty in February, 1252, just a few months before the
arrival of Thomas at Paris was an ominous warning of more
serious things to come. It was the opening gun of an all-out
war, not merely against the friars at Paris but against the
very existence of religious orders. The mendicants ignored
the warning and went about their business as usual, violently
attacking the doctrines of the secular professors, increasing
their hold on the people, reaping their benefactions, and

irking the lax consciences of the intellectuals by their personal mortification and sanctity.

Seeing that their public denunciation had no effect the professors started an undercover campaign of whispering and ridicule. Shady stories about the friars were passed from mouth to mouth; bawdy songs burlesquing their way of life were sung in taverns. When these devices failed in the desired effect because of the passivity of their objects the professors started a campaign of persecution. The large hoodlum element of the student body was incited by the secular party to persecute the friars. The religious were attacked on the streets and their convents were picketed and damaged. There were times when the students kept such a close watch on the Dominican and Franciscan houses that the inmates could not leave even for the purpose of obtaining food.

The strife was waged fiercely for several years marked by strikes and bitter publications on the part of the secular party and silence combined with dogged determination on the part of the regulars. Thomas Aquinas, meanwhile continued teaching at the university with marked success. If he took any part in the disputes up to this time there is no record of it. He became a fullfledged bachelor and was teaching and studying in preparation for the time he would be called to assume the doctor's cap. The riots of the students outside his convent probably did not even intrude upon his consciousness. He became notorious in later life for fits of abstraction even in the presence of high dignitaries of Church and State. That faculty of intense concentration was doubtless used to advantage at this hectic time.

There are a few strokes that should be added at this time to our gradually developing portrait of the man from Rocca Sicca. We have not yet described his physical appearance and Thomas, by this date (1254), had reached the perfection of his manhood. Considerably over six feet in height he had a huge frame emphasized by an inclination to corpulence.

We are told that he was so big that the peasants working in the fields gaped at him in wonderment when he passed. His skin was of dark golden hue, the "color of ripe wheat." When he walked his bearing was erect and gave the observer the impression of pride and strength. His head was large and bold in outline. In spite of the double chin and the general heaviness of feature owing to excess flesh his face did not give one the impression of slowness and stupidity so often given by big faces of that type, for the large, cloudless eyes, under the high forehead and the delicately arched eyebrows, drew the attention of the observer irresistibly to themselves. The eyes, which are so often indications of the mental capacity of the brain behind, gave no hint of the brilliance of Aquinas. In his case they were truly the windows of the soul. Thomas' eyes were calm, peaceful, and childlike. One was not struck so much by their expression as their lack of expression of positive emotional characteristics. The mouth below a straightly chiseled nose was full and of the type generally described as "sensitive."

It was probably at Paris during this period that Thomas first met Reginald of Piperno, a fellow Dominican, who became his companion for the remainder of his life and who also assumed the role of confessor and spiritual director of the saint. It is from Reginald's testimony that most of the little that is known of Thomas is derived. Historians have always bemoaned the fact that Reginald did not live long enough after the death of Thomas to write a full-length biography. Such a biography written by Reginald would probably not be of much value anyway for Thomas' companion evidently was convinced that only stories with a heavy accent on the miraculous or wonderful were worth relating. Practically everything related by him that has come down to us is in this vein. However, we should not belittle Brother Reginald of Piperno. Whatever his shortcomings as a scientific biographer he was invaluable to Thomas as a friend and aide.

From this period, also, and probably before he became embroiled in the university strife there is the little anecdote about Thomas on a hike with some of the students. The walk had taken them to St. Denis from which they had enjoyed a fine view of Paris. As they were returning to the city one of the students, who had been captivated by the view, remarked to Thomas, "Master, how beautiful is the city of Paris!" "Yes, indeed," answered Thomas, "it is a beautiful city." "If it only belonged to you," sighed the student. "And what," asked Thomas somewhat surprised, "should I do with it?" The ingenious scholar had the answer right on the tip of his tongue. "Why you could sell it to the king," he rejoined, "and with the proceeds you could build all the convents that the Dominicans need." Thomas, no doubt, considered this a most worthy use of the money accruing to him from the sale of Paris. But there was something he needed at that time more than the Dominicans needed convents and his next remark showed how much he yearned for it. "Well, as a matter of fact," he replied, "right now I would rather have Chrysostom's homilies upon the gospel of St. Matthew." This anecdote is typical of the life Aquinas led until he was drawn into the dispute that was raging round him. Once involved he fought with the deadliness that is characteristic of the man who loves peace and truth.

Chapter 10

St. Amour Versus Aquinas

THOMAS took his degree of bachelor at Paris. He had difficulty getting it because of the mounting opposition of the secular faculty. When the time came for him to take his master's along with the brilliant Franciscan, Bonaventure, the opposition was so bitter that the granting of the well-merited honor had to be postponed. Neither Thomas nor Bonaventure had contributed to the mendicant cause by their popularity as teachers. Both were the talk of the university and students flocked to their lectures. Thomas' fame was spreading and it was during this period that he wrote his first theological work, *Commentary on the Sentences.*

The storm clouds that had been gathering around the University of Paris, emitting a low rumble of thunder and dim flash of lightening now and then, broke in full fury in 1255, when William of St. Amour assumed the leadership of the secular party, wrote his incendiary tract, *De Periculis Novissimis — The Dangers of the Last Days —* in 1255. In his philippic St. Amour attacked, with unchecked violence, the mendicant orders, particularly, the Dominicans. But St. Amour was too much imbued with the irreligion and the rationalistic spirit of the university to stop there. He went on to challenge the rights of the orders to existence.

In the opening paragraph of his slanderous tract St. Amour protests the purity of his motives. It is his intention merely to warn the Church that the signs which Christian prophets

foretold would precede the destruction of the world had
appeared. He avers that these were the signs alluded to by
Saint Paul in the third chapter of his *Second Epistle to
Timothy*, in the words: "Know also this, that in the last
days, shall come dangerous times. Men shall become lovers
of themselves, covetous, haughty, proud, blasphemers, dis-
obedient to parents, ungrateful, wicked." In fact, says St.
Amour, these men, possessing all the evil characteristics
designated by Paul in the ominous third chapter of the epistle
are living among us. They are none else than these
dissemblers who go about with the mien of piety and
meekness, these whited sepulchers who have the appearance
of godliness, which the Apostle of the Gentiles warned they
would possess, but who were, as Paul foretold they would
be, "traitors, stubborn, puffed up, and lovers of pleasure more
than God." These hypocrites are the mendicant friars.

According to St. Amour the very life they lead is against
the inspired teaching of Saint Paul and it is the Church's
duty, as the guardian of truth, to amputate this parasitic
growth which she has knowingly permitted to attach itself
to her body. Unless quick and vigorous steps are taken to
destroy it, warns the prophet of Paris, this incubus will
be the death of the Church. William declared that the friars
lived in constant sin, because it is a mortal sin to beg; and
not only that, but they were the constant occasion of sin to
others, because it is a mortal sin for anyone to give them an
alms. The Popes and bishops who allowed them to preach
and hear confessions without the consent of the parochial
clergy were also guilty of sin. All these propositions the
sanctimonious St. Amour supported by liberal quotations
from Holy Writ and the Fathers of the Church.

The devil, says Shakespeare, can quote Scripture for his
purpose and the bard of the Avon goes on to stigmatize an
evil soul producing holy witness as like a villain with a
smiling cheek; a goodly apple rotten at the heart. The great

English poet could not have given a better description of William of St. Amour had he been his roommate. The Parisian doctor cared nothing for the health or life of the Church. He probably did not believe in the Divine authority of the Scriptures he so glibly quoted. Historians express serious doubt that this self-appointed defender of the Faith was even a Christian. One of the large group of Parisian professors who had been corrupted by Arabian philosophy, William came to his new task with an unsavory record. His heretical opinions and unorthodox teaching had already brought upon him the unwelcome attention of the Bishop of Paris and the King of France. Some writers believe that in donning the armour of the white knight defending the integrity of Mother Church, he was drawing the red herring across his own pungent trail to throw the Pope's hounds off the scent. If that was his intention he was supinely stupid, for new heresy is not apt to improve a record blotched with old heresy and William must have known that the ground upon which he trod was dangerous. It seems more probable that St. Amour's attack on the regulars was inspired by his intense party feeling, a deep and undying hatred of the regulars.

The first answer that came to the secular champion's attack was a work that was as viciously false as his own. This tract, titled *Introduction to the Eternal Gospel*, was written, it appears, by some Franciscan. The writer's intention was to glorify the religious life but his head was not equal to the dictates of his heart for his treatise is crammed with theological error. Bonaventure must have almost died with shame and sorrow when he read it and wondered how it was possible that a Catholic let alone a Franciscan could have been responsible for it.

These two works brought all the bad blood at the university once more to the boiling point. The palpable blasphemy and heresy contained in the *Introduction to the*

Eternal Gospel gave St. Amour and his coterie the opportunity they had been looking for. They now posed as crusaders who, on behalf of holy Church, were intent upon stamping out these heretics. Persecution of the mendicants was renewed. Meanwhile, both St. Amour's pamphlet and that authored by the anonymous Franciscan were sent to the Pope for judgment by Louis IX, King of France. The Pope who was then at Anagni summoned before him representatives of both the regular and the secular parties. It was the intention of Alexander IV to judge more than the books. Among those sent to represent the regulars were Thomas, Albert, and Bonaventure. The friars made certain that they were not going to lose the argument for want of talent to represent their cause. The secular faculty was likewise well represented, their cause being defended by William of St. Amour, Odo of Douais, Christian of Beauvais, Nicholas of Bar sur Aube, John Belin, and the Englishman, John of Gecteville. The book was to go on trial before a court composed of four cardinals, namely, Eudes de Chatteauroux, John Franciago, Hugh of St. Cher, and John of Ursini.

The regulars made no attempt to save the *Introduction to the Eternal Gospel* from condemnation; they concentrated their efforts on obtaining the decision of the court against St. Amour's pernicious work and defending the right of the friars to existence. That decision was a surety if anything ever was. Probably nowhere before or since in the history of the world has any cause been so ably defended and in no court has there appeared at the same time talent equal to the combined brilliance of these three men. The sessions opened before the arrival of the Paris delegation. After hearing the devastating argumentation presented by the friars, the cardinals did not think it worth their while to even wait for the secular advocates. They recommended to the Pope that the book be immediately condemned. On October 18, 1256, Alexander IV published the bull, *Quasi Lignum Vitae,*

in which the entire work was damned as criminal and in-
iquitous and all possessing copies of it were ordered to burn
the same within eight days under the pain of excommunication. The forbidden book was burned publicly in the presence
of the Pope, October 23.

The secular delegation arrived to find that their cause had
already been lost. They instituted an appeal without delay
and were directed by the Pope to subscribe to the terms of
the bull or suffer the consequences. Odo of Douais and
Christian of Beauvais both took the required oath. They likewise promised, under oath, to receive the friars among the
faculty of the university, to combat any attempt to break up
the mendicant schools, and to preach in defense of the
principles of the Religious state. St. Amour refused to subscribe to the oaths; so he was forbidden, under the pain of
excommunication, to return to France. Under the threat of
the same penalty he was to refrain from teaching or writing.
As a punishment for his intransigent attitude, he was deprived
of several benefices which he held. St. Amour retired to his
estates in Burgundy to sulk but he did not let his hatred
die nor did he give up the fight. He managed to return to
Paris in 1263 and he started anew to stir up antagonism to
the regulars. As a matter of fact the sentence of the Pope
did not settle the matter forever. The opposition to the friars
continued secretly as we shall see.

Thomas is supposed to have prepared his great work,
Contra Impugnantes Dei Cultum, generally known as *The
Defense of Religious Orders* in the convent at Anagni
in a few days in compliance with the orders of Humberto de
Romanis, the Dominican Master General. The work is
divided into three parts. In the first part Thomas teaches the
origin, essence, and perfection of the religious life and the
various reasons for which the Church can institute or sanction
an order. The second part discusses the arguments of St.
Amour and gives the true sense of the numerous passages

from Scripture and the Fathers quoted by him and twisted to his purpose. Proving that he was also at home in the practical world and away from the rarefied atmosphere of the metaphysical, Thomas, in the third part of the work, treats the concrete charges hurled by St. Amour against the regulars and proves them false. His tract is considered the best defense of the religious life ever written. The work done by Albert and the two tracts of Bonaventure, *On the Poverty of Christ* and *In Defense of the Poor* cannot be lightly pushed aside but it was Thomas, says Archbishop Vaughn, "whose exceptional grasp embraced the entire religious question; and his genius it was which replaced the fundamental principles of the highest love of God in their old position of reverence and honor; and, in achieving this result the Angelical Doctor left to all coming generations the most profound refutation of deadly error, and the most masterly exposition of religious truth, which has ever been given to the world by any Doctor of the Church."

Chapter 11

Thomas the Teacher

THOMAS did not tarry long at Anagni. After the case had been fought and won he returned almost immediately to Paris, narrowly escaping shipwreck on the way. The blow struck by the Pope at the secular party had had its effect in Paris; and Thomas, arriving there, found that the university was now disposed to confer the mastership upon him and Bonaventure. Both received the degree at the close of 1256 from Eimerich, the chancellor of the university. Nevertheless, the secular faculty were not disposed to receive either of them for a while.

As Master of Sacred Theology, Thomas could now teach sacred science on his own authority. For three years longer he remained in Paris and his popularity and fame as a teacher increased with the passing time. During this period he produced the treatise *De Veritate,* considered one of his greatest works, and his commentaries on the *Gospel of Saint Matthew* and the *De Trinitate of Boethius.* He was not the ordinary, humdrum professor who was as common in Paris then as he has been in all schools in all ages. Thomas brought to the study and teaching of theology that freshness of viewpoint, that insatiable curiosity which are generally associated with research laboratories of physical science but hardly ever with the classroom of theology. "He brought up new questions," says one of his biographers, "inaugurated a new and valuable method of research and demonstration and developed new arguments. Those who heard him resolving difficulties and problems in a new way, with new principles, believed that he had been endowed by God with a new light of understanding."

Bartholomew of Lucca, a contemporary, calls him the "ark of philosophy and theology." John of Colonna styles him the "incomparable teacher." From all sides, even from enemies like Siger de Brabant and Godfrey of Fontaines, came praise in the highest terms for the genius of Aquinas. Thomas saw the weaknesses in the theological system of his day and he set about to correct them. The principal weakness of that system was a fear of the use of reason. Orthodox theology was taught from the authoritarian standpoint. Augustine says so and so, Dionysius, speaks thusly; Chrysostom, Ambrose, Basil, Gregory — all these were quoted; the authority of Holy Scripture was cited voluminously but no attempt was made to defend authority with reason. *Credo ut intelligam* was the watchword of the schools.

This had not always been the case. Augustine had attempted to draw up a rationalistic system of theology and had failed only because the best philosophy he could find on which to base his system was faulty. The Christianized Platonism of Augustine was, at best, a makeshift. A creed as real as is Christianity could never be adequately guarded by the shadow soldiery of Plato. In the time of Augustine, Aristotle was being tortured in his eastern prison. The Stagyrite was not yet ready for baptism.

St. Anselm, in his day, made a valiant effort to reconcile Faith and reason, and considering the odds against which he fought his success was immense. Owing to his efforts the disguise which had been forced on reason to make it appear an enemy of Faith was partially removed. By the time Anselm finished washing the face of the poor captive, behold! there for the world to see was a being that bore some resemblance to the glorious, resplendent Faith. Surely this was not an enemy but some poor relation who, by a tragic case of mistaken identity, had been held captive for many years. Had Anselm possessed the magic formula he could have removed the rest of the disguise and shown Reason to the world as she truly was — a beautiful woman who had no peer and no superior but her glorious sister, Faith. But Aristotle, the benign magician who alone possessed the formula, was still held prisoner in Araby. The prince to whom that favor was granted was Thomas, who clad in shining armor, attacked the Arabians and freed the captive magician. Surely if St. Francis can be called the knight errant of Lady Poverty, Thomas with as much reason can be called the champion of Lady Reason.

When Thomas started teaching at Paris the methods of teaching theology had declined from the glorious days of Anselm. It had been many, many years since the Church had produced an Augustine, an Anselm, or a Bernard. The rationalistic systems established by these giants had been badly battered. The superstructure had been riddled and now the foundation stones were bearing the brunt of the cannonade. And the reason why these princely palaces were falling was because Aristotle had come out of the East. But the Aristotle who appeared in Europe at this time was not the Aristotle whom the Arabians had made prisoner. Long years of captivity had changed his appearance. He wore Arabian dress and his face and figure were wild and unkempt. In the once calm eyes there was the fixed stare of the irrational mystic. But his devastating intellect retained its cunning and its great gift for dialectic. Entirely under the power of his captors he used his eloquent, biting tongue to support their fantastic arguments. Working skillfully at the command of his masters principally Avincenna, Avenpace, and Averöes, he made short work of the Christian systems which had been based upon the philosophy of Plato at whose feet Aristotle, in the dim past, had sat as disciple.

The Christian theologians forsook their beautiful but

delicate castles and retired to the plain but stout fortress of authority. And this was the state of the Christian schools when Thomas came to Paris. Thomas was not content to remain cooped up in the narrow confines of the fortress. To his fighting nature the inactivity was nerve racking. He thought that a counterattack should be made to capture Aristotle. Thomas believed that the Stagyrite once captured and brought back to his true sense would be the savior of Christianity. To this task he dedicated his life.

To the stodgy authoritarian professors of Paris Thomas was an anomaly. A professor of theology on the world's foremost faculty, this young upstart was obviously a freethinker. He publicly proclaimed that to him human authority, no matter who that authority happened to be, was not the highest source of truth next to revelation. If someone quoted the great St. Augustine against him on some point, Thomas waved aside the authority and demanded reasonable proof for Augustine's statement. To Thomas it was not who said it but what he said that carried the greatest weight. Such an attitude caused as much consternation in the thirteenth century as it would in the twentieth. The great difference between our own century and the thirteenth is that the stuffy minds of that age demanded that the authority at least be worthy of respect. Today mouths gape and eyes pop with attention every time some successful manufacturer or actress advances an opinion on theology and, of course, any one who would dream of contradicting a great scientist when he speaks of God would be considered an arrant fool.

Thomas did not disdain authority; he merely examined its statements. So great was his respect for Augustine that when, in his writings, he is forced to contradict him he always respectfully tips his hat before doing so and then corrects him so gently and with such finesse that the reader gets the impression that Augustine really meant to say what Thomas has said for him. But the professors at Paris were not to be

misled by this professed respect for authority. This young upstart scoffed the authority of the great teachers. He had the
supreme effrontery to contradict Augustine, Anselm, Jerome,
Ambrose, and the rest despite his professed reverence for
them. He revered Aristotle, the philosopher of the heretics.
To them it seemed that his respect for the pagan Greek
was much more profound and real than for the great
Christian doctors. Here, indeed, was the devil in the guise
of a monk — an extremely clever devil who had dedicated
himself to the corruption of the spouse of Christ. He must
be watched, spies must be sent to hang on his lips, his
writings must be examined minutely. The professors had
determined to trap Thomas in his speech as another stuffy-
minded group long before had determined to trap his Master.

Chapter 12

Thomas the Saint

PERHAPS the principle reason for Thomas' success as a teacher, writes Jacques Maritain, the French philosopher, was that he lived the doctrine he taught. And the same writer points out that none of the immense labor that occupied Thomas as teacher, preacher, and writer distracted him from his interior life because all of that labor dealt with God and was consecrated to His greater glory. In the classroom, in the pulpit, and at his desk, he was teaching the same doctrine in a different dress. The scientific exposition of the classroom was pruned of excess verbiage and illustrations by the pen, simplified and fitly clothed with imagery when it was given to Christ's little ones from the pulpit.

Work not directly connected with the office of teaching the word of God was somewhat brusquely pushed aside by Thomas even though that work were offered him by a king. For although some writers state that Thomas acted as director to his kinsman, St. Louis of France, in the affairs of state it appears more probable that Thomas declined the proffered position. Biographers of Thomas have gone to great lengths to prove that the period Thomas was in Paris coincides with the most successful period of the crusader-king's reign and they ascribe the success to the counsel of Thomas. No doubt, Thomas did give the benefit of his wisdom to the king to the latter's profit but it seems equally certain that Louis consulted Thomas only on occasions and as a last court of appeal in more difficult cases. Being a saint himself, the French monarch would hesitate to summon a saint too often to a royal court and away from the work he had to do.

However, Aquinas was proof against the uproar of the court when he had something upon his mind in the nature of a problem, which was practically all of the time. The biographers relate that on one occasion when Thomas and the prior of St. James were dining with the king and queen and a few guests, Thomas became suddenly concerned with one such problem. He had been recently writing a paper against the Manichean heretics and he had been absorbed in the question when the prior dragged him off to the banquet. Oblivious to his surroundings he fell into a state of abstraction and thrashed out the problem. Suddenly, to the surprise of the entire company he shouted, as he pounded the table, "At last I have the clinching argument against the Manicheans." The mortified prior, who was sitting by the side of Thomas, plucked his sleeve and admonished him to remember where he was. But the king smilingly brushed aside the prior's profuse apologies and ordered that secretaries be summoned to take the saint's dictation lest the argument be lost.

This anecdote is not the only one illustrating his powers of abstraction. According to Reginald, Thomas, although he was supersensitive to pain, had only to contemplate on the things of God when he had to pay a visit to the leech to become thoroughly unaware of what was going on including the pain of the operation. At table it was Reginald's task to see that Thomas ate his meals because if he became concerned with some problem he forgot to eat. Incidentally, there seems to be no foundation to the story, which is the only thing about Thomas that some people know, namely, that because of his great girth it was necessary to cut out a piece of the refectory table.

Thomas' huge size has also counted against him in the minds of better informed people. Because one does not usually associate corpulence with an ascetic the impression is received that Thomas was a merry monk addicted to the pleasures of the table and not much given to mortification and fasting. The truth is that Thomas' size was entirely natural and he retained it in spite of his fasting and penances. Thomas lived the strict Dominican rule as it was practiced throughout the Order in those days of first fervor and vigor. Had he done no more he would have qualified as an ascetic. Perhaps castigation of the body is not closely associated with his name because that form of penance is a necessity to the apostolic man rather than to the teacher and writer. "The crucifixion of the pen" is a penance as arduous as castigation because the constant effort required to curb the body's natural urge to activity achieves the same end.

That Thomas lived the ascetical life is proved by the fact that he achieved the end for which the ascetic strives — union with God. The gift of contemplation he had, as we have already shown, to a high degree. "His gift of prayer," writes William of Tocco, "exceeded all bounds; he raised himself to God as freely as though no burden of flesh held him back. Not a day passed that he was not ravished out of his senses." He often wept during the celebration of Mass and at the chanting of compline during Lent he could never hear the antiphon *"ne projicias nos in tempore senectutis cum defecerit virtus nostra ne derelinquas nos, Domine"* — "Cast us not off in our old age, O Lord, when our strength is declining do not abandon us" — without bursting into tears.

According to Reginald he was the recipient of extraordinary favors. Once when doubts seized him as to the purity of the doctrine of this new theology which he was introducing, Our Lady appeared to him to reassure and encourage him to persevere in his trail blazing. At another time, and this is also according to Reginald's sworn testimony, Thomas was baffled by an obscure passage in the course of his commentary on Isaias completed during this period at Paris. He resorted to his usual practice when confronted by a seemingly insuper-able difficulty, that of fasting and praying. This he continued for several days and then one night Reginald heard him talking to someone in his room. Finally the conversation ceased and Thomas called Reginald to his cell and bade him take dictation. For an hour he discoursed on the passage that had previously challenged all explanation, giving a lucid solution to the apparent insoluble problem; then he told Reginald to return to bed. But Reginald, determined to find out the identity of the mysterious nocturnal visitors, fell on his knees before Thomas and begged to know who owned the voices he had heard. After first swearing his friend to secrecy, Thomas revealed to him that he had been visited by St. Peter and St. Paul who had cleared up the difficulty that had faced him.

Many moderns, even modern Catholics are inclined to receive such stories with their tongues in their cheeks and as far as defined Faith goes Catholics have the privilege of rejecting anecdotes of this type. Yet if we reject them, in this case, we are faced with one of two alternatives neither of which are flattering to that good friar, Brother Reginald of Piperno. Either Reginald was an outrageous liar or the simplest of simple fools and there is no foundation for either assumption. We will not relate, in this work all the miracles and wonders told of Thomas. The reader interested in such hagiography can easily obtain it.[Thomas the saint, Thomas the scholar, Thomas the preacher, Thomas the teacher, all these qualities of the man from Rocca Sicca have been extensively treated. But Thomas the man has been too much neglected. And this task cannot be adequately fulfilled, the picture will be incomplete, unless all sides of the man are studied. Therefore, all these phases must be touched upon but none stressed. The man from Rocca Sicca has been hidden too long in the shadow of the *Summa*.]

Thomas had a very busy day every day. He rose very

early in the morning and celebrated Mass. Then he served
the Mass of some other priest while he made thanksgiving
for his own. For the rest of the day the schedule was
simplicity itself. When not lecturing or praying he was
writing. He took his brief recreation on working days walking alone and fast with head up in the cloister corridors.
This duty occupied him, usually, for fifteen or twenty
minutes. He was a man with a great task to perform, the
complete reorganization of the Catholic system of thought,
and he had no time to waste precious hours in idle, or at
best, nonproductive talk. With the exception of this capacity
for work he had few eccentricities. He is reported to have
been very affable and gentle with a low, well-modulated
voice. He seems to have been ready to help anybody at any
time whether within the convent or without. No one evidently held him in awe or feared him. Apparently no one
who knew him disliked him as a man although many disliked
his methods in teaching and writing and opposed him bitterly
in these spheres. He most certainly was not an ordinary man
but he never gave anyone the impression that he was
supernatural. He left it for posterity to do that and posterity
did it well. The man can't be seen for his books.

Chapter 13

Thomas the Man

WE have pointed out in a previous chapter that Thomas has been unfortunate in his biographers. His best friend, Reginald of Piperno, who was the only one in a position to be his Boswell, never wrote a formal biography. But from what little information he did leave we can say that it is just as well he did not because Reginald obviously believed that the less of the human element admitted in a great man the more of a hero and model he would be. Reginald in his revelations concerning Thomas had a weather eye cocked on the reading public and the reading public of the middle ages definitely did not want their saints to be too human. They wanted their saints to show forth the grace of God because to them that was what counted to the exclusion of everything else. William of Tocco and Bernard Guy, the two earliest biographers of Thomas, also wrote from this standpoint. And the man from Rocca Sicca has been equally unfortunate in later and even contemporary biographers. Sertillanges, Maritain, Gilson, Grabmann, and Vann, all capable scholars, have been interested in Thomas as a philosopher and theologian and their works are admirable expositions of the Thomistic system but they make little effort to materialize the man behind the system, because as theologians their chief interest lay in the system. The great G. K. Chesterton who could write well on everything or nothing missed the boat on his attempt to picture Thomas. Those who read G. K.'s *Thomas Aquinas* expecting to find therein a new portrait were confronted with the old familiar picture of the great thinker.

In our day of streamlined hagiography, when books come pouring off the presses throwing new light on old saints and infusing the straw figures of the early biographers with rich red blood, when the secret of this saint and the humanity of that are entertainingly revealed by gifted writers, Thomas Aquinas has remained the king of shadows. To those who know his name he is still the *Angelic Doctor,* the *Angel of the Schools, Divus Thomas,* the *Prince of Theologians* — all justly merited titles, all showing his glory after a fashion, but all unsympathetic and superhuman. There is nothing sympathetic from the viewpoint of ordinary human relationship, about an unattached intellect, be it the greatest that ever existed, and it is not apt to twang the cords of our hearts. The general public realizes that Thomas is a great saint but he is not the saint that John Jones prays to. Sarah Smith knows that Thomas holds a high position on the altars — why there are even churches under his patronage — but when Sarah Smith prays she chooses a human, appealing, proletarian saint like the Little Flower or John Bosco who had to struggle for their salvation even as you and I; saints who knew heartbreak and joy; saints who laughed and wept because they had human emotions. John and Sarah may admire the *Angel of the Schools,* they may be in awe when told of the wonders accomplished by the great unattached intellect but they are content to be in awe and admire from the distance. They have no desire to get up close to Thomas for they are certain to feel uncomfortable in the presence of this acme of perfection.

Now, the irony of the situation is this: none of the writers who have written on Thomas intended to take him away from the people. Neither Reginald of Piperno nor William of Tocco nor Bernard Guy nor any of the older biographers desired such a calamity. We have already stated that these three definitely had an eye on the public when they wrote, and the public of the middle ages received Thomas enthusiastically. The *Angelic Warfare* under the patronage of Saint Thomas was one of the most popular devotions in the Church. Where the early writers failed was in putting such a low value upon human qualities that they refused to record them so that later biographers writing for a public whose standards had changed could present an appealing picture to their times.

Of course it would be an impossibility to present any saint in an appealing light to the modern pagan world which values only animal, mineral, or vegetative perfections. To that world huge muscles, white teeth, long eyelashes and curly hair and, perhaps, a fast line of double talk would recommend any character. As a matter of fact part of the Little Flower's great appeal in our day lies in the fact that she was "pretty." But the Christian world, although it may be prejudiced in favor of the *Little Flower* because she was pretty and a bit cold toward Saint Alexis and Benedict Labre because they were dirty, and although it may place less value upon the gifts of grace and more value upon the human characteristics of a saint, still realizes that it is the grace of God that counts and that human characteristics to be of any value must be truly human not merely animal or worse. To this public Thomas should appeal as much as he did to their medieval forefathers because Thomas was very human.

The writer is tempted in presenting Thomas to the modern world to stress three qualities highly valued today. Thomas was a tremendous man, endowed with great physical strength. It would not be too difficult to play up this quality in such a way as to make him a hands-down favorite as the patron saint of football. His life had its adventurous side because for twenty years he covered several of the countries of Europe on foot. He tramped over the romantic Alps several times facing all the difficulties and dangers involved in such a trip, getting his food where he could find it and sleeping at night anywhere he could obtain hospitality. With his great size and noble head, regular features, and large eyes he was surely a handsome man — all these so-called human characteristics might be stressed in presenting Thomas to the modern world. But that would not be Thomas. Any writer in so catering to an age would be making a greater mistake than did the early biographers. They, too, showed only one side of Thomas, God's side, they neglected the human qualities to bring out the divine quality, but how much better that is than to neglect the human side to stress the animal.

There is no saint who does not possess human attractiveness. No old saw was ever less true than the saying that saints are all right but not to live with. The only one who would find it difficult to live with a real saint is the devil or one who is considerably under his control. Thomas' sanctity is a proof of his humanity. Probably the most common and most unattractive human vice is selfishness. The utterly selfish man is incapable of loving anyone because he is head over heels in love with himself. A man of this type is unattractive because he is impossible to live with. The saint is most lovable because he has less love of self. Thomas was most unselfish. The determined and successful fight he made against his inherited tendency to pride proves that. He could have been the shining light among his fellows because of his intellectual gifts. Thomas chose to hide these gifts and be "the dumb ox." The very nickname he was given proves that he was likable. His brethren may have considered him the convent simpleton but he was thought to be a lovable fool because no one is going around calling a man of Thomas' size and strength names that man is likely to resent. The name the brethren gave him and the fact that they made him the butt of their jokes does not make him seem a hard man to live with.

Thomas knew suffering though he probably kept it to himself. The insistent appeals his family made to him to abandon his vocation when he was at Cologne must have pulled at his heart strings. Thomas' loyalty to his sisters throughout his life shows that he possessed a deep family feeling. What, then, must have been his suffering on hearing of the fate that had befallen his brothers? The mere physical sufferings that were a part of his everyday life were nothing in comparison.

The impression has come down through the centuries that Thomas, the great intellect, was cut off from all social intercourse with his fellow men. That simply could not be. No friar was so separated from the people — the friars were of the people; in that fact lay the secret of their success. And Thomas in his many, many journeys met a great many people. On the road, in inns, at homes where food was begged — everywhere there were people — people who would run and hide, possibly, at the sight of My Lord Bishop, people who would be a bit afraid of a monk, people who would be abashed in the presence of the parish priest; but afraid of a friar with whom they shared their food — never. Thomas traveled a great deal and Thomas begged his food. How could social contact have been avoided? But possibly in his contact with people the great intellect munched his food in silence or went off into a trance! Then where did he gather the material for his numerous sermons? Where did he get the deep insight into human nature with its hopes, loves, and fears, its grappling with the problems of everyday existence, that he shows in the *Summa*. These things were not grabbed out of thin air or deduced by *a priori* reasoning. Thomas' range of acquaintances was broad, all the way from beggars to kings.

The great philosopher was not above the little amenities of life. His affection for Reginald to whom he dedicated one of his opuscula and for whom he wrote his *Compendium* shows us a man who was both loving and lovable. It is revealed by the anecdote relating what Thomas did with the present sent him by his sister, the Countess Morisco. The Countess sent her brother a gift of money. Thomas in turning it over to the Prior requested, as a special favor, that the students be given a feast. This special regard for the young was characteristic of Thomas. At the peak of his career, when he was the ablest teacher in Christendom and his services were in great demand by his Order and his Church, Thomas found time to write a book for beginners so that the young students of theology would find their task an easier one. A great American Thomist has compared Thomas doing this to "Paderewski teaching scales." One of the very rare occasions when Thomas roared like a bull in anger was when he observed the Averroists corrupting the youth at the University of Paris with their sly, sophistical teaching. This sneaking cowardice brought upon them the withering scorn of Aquinas. He challenged them to put their doctrine in writing and defend it in the open before men and not hand it out in classrooms to boys who were not able to defend themselves.

There are many examples of Thomas' warm humanity to be found in the *Summa Theologica* itself. Contained in that great work which is a model of cool, scientific, objective writing, there are observations that could have been penned only by a man who knew life and who had a deep under-standing of and greatest sympathy for human nature in all its vagaries. For instance, in treating of the birth of Christ, Thomas treats the entire question in minute detail. He discusses the angels, the star, the Magi, the cave, the Virgin — all at great length. The task of writing on this event with all its human appeal he evidently relishes. But when he comes to treat of the Passion of Christ, he crowds the whole heart-rending story into two articles. Thomas found the task of commenting on the death of his Friend and Master too much for him.

The *Summa* is full of common sense and sympathy, for

all its reputation as a dry, metaphysical work. In discussing the best means to alleviate sorrow, the great intellect proscribes a very sane treatment, namely, a good sleep and a bath. Asking the question: what should be done with a person who wants to weep? Thomas replies: let him weep because if he really wants to weep, nothing would afford him equal pleasure at that time. The most hopeful people in the world, according to Thomas, are the young and the intoxicated, the first because they have so little experience with failure, the second because they have succeeded in drowning theirs. Concerning the universal problem of getting the most fun out of life, Thomas advises work because, he says, fun is a relaxation from work and a preparation for work. Without work it is impossible to have fun. What did the great metaphysician think of the art of the cosmetician? Standing alone against the opinion of the Fathers, all of whom branded it as a sin of some sort, Aquinas refused to regard it as evil in itself. He opined that for a good reason it could be permitted. Thomas thought that a girl should present her best face to the public and stay in the running. A married woman could employ the art to keep her husband interested.

These are but a few of the observations of a man who, in common opinion, had ice water for blood — and these are but a few. This work is not a commentary on the *Summa* even for the purpose of showing its more human and hidden side. It is regrettable that the early biographers did not leave us a clear picture of the very human person who made them. The more detailed and concrete sketch which they could have drawn would have revealed to us, beyond doubt, a man who was a charming personality.

Chapter 14

Preacher and Poet

ANOTHER side of the versatile man from Rocca Sicca that has been obscured by his fame as a theologian is his ability in the pulpit. He was one of the outstanding and most popular preachers of his time. It is generally presumed that great theologians are poor preachers. Very often they are, but that is not owing to the fact that they are great theologians. Barring speech defects, the theologian who is not a preacher has allowed something to happen to his humanity. The old excuse that scientific study has stultified his imagination is a lame one and the equally old excuse that he can't express his science in the popular speech is likewise crippled. If his spiritual life is all that it should be and his humanity has not been warped by selfish seclusion the good theologian should excel as a preacher. Thomas, being not only a great theologian, was a saint and, therefore, a great man. The sum of these qualities is the great preacher.

The opinion has been expressed by a noted Dominican writer that St. Thomas knew only one language, Latin, in addition to his native Italian. He supports this statement by pointing out that all of the sermons and sermon outlines written by Thomas are in that language. If this were a fact then all of Thomas' preaching would have been to the clergy for in Thomas' time this was the only group to which sermons were preached in the official language of the Church. The sermons to the people were preached in the vulgar tongue, although the outlines for these sermons and often the sermons themselves were written in Latin. Now it is a certainty that Thomas preached to the people of three countries: Italy, Germany, and France. He was a popular preacher and crowds flocked to hear him. The only safe conclusion is that Thomas could speak the three languages and speak them well — an additional argument, incidentally, for the fact that he mixed with the people. He certainly never learned French and German in the Dominican convents where the official tongue was Latin.

Thomas began his preaching career at Cologne either shortly before or shortly after ordination. The people liked the fire, simplicity, and zeal of the young preacher and crowds came to hear him. Like all big men his appearance favored him. The sight of his huge frame topped by the striking head in the pulpit, predisposed his audience to hear what he had to say. And Aquinas never lost their attention. His sermons were marked by simplicity, depth, and balance. The power he possessed over an audience was almost hypnotic. Touron gives an illustration of this. While he was speaking in St. Peter's in Rome on one occasion on the Passion of Christ, so striking was his language and so vividly did he present the picture that the congregation wept so loudly that Thomas was forced to halt in the midst of his discourse. On Easter Sunday following, his sermon on the triumph of Christ so stirred the audience that he had to stop once more while the people cheered.

As a preacher Thomas was animated but not theatrical. He depended, it would seem, more upon the power of his words, the vividness of his imagery, and the genuine depth of his own emotions to teach and instruct his hearers, to make them see what he saw and feel what he felt. The sermon outlines of Thomas constitute one of the opuscula. There are one hundred and forty-two for Sundays and eighty-three for feast days. It is very probable that Thomas with his day-in, day-out experience as a lecturer needed no more

than these outlines in order to preach a sermon. It is not
likely that he wrote out the entire sermon. The outlines are,
as one would expect them to be, masterpieces of their kind.

That the sermons which he developed from these and
other outlines were also great can be concluded from the
fact that he was the outstanding Dominican preacher of his
time and that is saying a great deal for in the art of preaching
the sons of Dominic, as a group, were unsurpassed. "The
Dominicans were, without doubt," says Archbishop Vaughn,
"the great preachers of the thirteenth century. In 1273, sixty
preachers were employed in the principal churches of Paris,
and of them, exactly one half were Dominicans." Thomas
preached, as we have said, in Rome, Cologne, and Paris
but probably no city heard him more often than Naples,
where he preached frequently over a period of ten years.
There he preached an entire course of sermons during one
Lent on the single text "Ave Maria gratia plena, Dominus
tecum," the first part of the angelic salutation. William of
Tocco tells us that the people reverenced his word as if it
came directly from the mouth of Christ.

The picture of Thomas in the pulpit, with his great frame
alive and animated, his magnificent head moving to emphasize
his points, the deep calm eyes sparkling with fire that burned
within as he preached Christ and Him crucified; this picture
of a Thomas whose burning words and vivid imagery could
move his audience to tears; this is not the Thomas of popular
imagination — the great theologian and metaphysician, the
dry-as-dust professor who could speak only in syllogisms.
This strange being is a popular preacher, a man who could
move the masses, who could make the little ones of Christ
weep or cheer. This, indeed, is the unknown Thomas.

The poetry of Aquinas is fairly well known. Most of it
has been put to music and part of it is sung in the Catholic
churches of the world every time the Blessed Sacrament is
exposed. It is genuine poetry, not mere rhyme and has drawn

praise from literary men of all ages, most of whom not knowing the real Thomas, have expressed great surprise that such
burning words, such fine expression of genuine poetic passion
should have come from the pen of a famous theologian. Well,
as a matter of fact, there is no reason why a great theologian
cannot be a great poet just as there is no good reason why
he cannot be a great preacher. Provided he has the gifts
necessary for a poet, the fact that he is a theologian should
be a help rather than a hindrance.

There is one very different thing about the poetry of
Aquinas. It probably never would have been written had the
Pope not ordered him to write it. Every line of it concerns
the Holy Eucharist and it was all written for the one
occasion — the institution of the Feast of Corpus Christi. That
was characteristic of Thomas. Most of his great works in
theology were written either at the orders of his superior or
at the dictates of his own conscience because he saw their
great need. Now, his poetry was all written by command.
He would never have written it simply for self-expression.
And it was not merely good, workmanlike poetry. It was great
poetry that proved the writer to be a poetic genius. Gounod,
the famous French musician, said he would gladly exchange
all the music he had written to have been the author of the
Preface of the Mass of Corpus Christi. Yet the great poet
never wrote another line of poetry. Simply because he had
other and more important things to do.

Some of the long-haired Bohemians who go about with
a languid air and world-weary expression, because they think
that this is the way a genuine poet is supposed to be, would
deny to Thomas the right to the title of poet because (they
would say) had he been a true poet the spontaneous urge
to sing could not have been suppressed any more than a
bird's. Well without going into a discussion of free will with
those who cultivate eccentricity because it is the easiest way
to attract attention, let it be said that singing can be done

in more than one tune and Thomas never stopped singing.
He sang in the pulpit and every article of the *Summa* is a
poem, or rather stanzas of one great epic — the ineffable
wonders of God and the unutterable gifts that he has
bestowed upon man.

To Thomas the poetic form was just another means of
expressing this wonderful idea. To him poetry and poets are
not things apart from the rest of mankind to be treated, the
poem with wondering awe and the poet with special reverence. To Thomas the poet was a creature with special gifts
from God, enabling him to say beautiful things in a beautiful
way but no reason for being an object of special reverence.
Thomas expresses in his poetry, in a more delicate way, the
same sentiments he expresses in the *Summa*. "The poet," says
Sertillanges, "is an intuitive philosopher, the philosopher a
reflecting poet." But Thomas was no mere poet as he was
no mere philosopher. As a poet his creative genius made him
an innovator and pathfinder, also. By his novel use of stress
and rhythm in his Eucharistic hymns he broke away from
the ancient rules of prosody and approached modern
standards.

Thomas as a poet remained the philosopher. Not for him
were the airy emptiness and sweet nothings of those singers
whose muse is beautiful but dumb. The great metaphysician
was no "metaphysical" poet. His lyre was strung with strong,
tough strings. He sang of the things that surpass all understanding but he sang of them in a down-to-earth, concrete
way — *vere panis filiorum non mittendus canibus*. With swift
imagery, in the *Pange Lingua* he covers the same ground as
several tracts in theology and in a manner that is almost as
satisfying to the intellect. The *Lauda Sion*, more discursive,
considers not only the Holy Eucharist itself but the reasons
for and the circumstances surrounding its institution. It, too,
presents the truths it teaches in striking images and exhibits
a marvelous power in the use of words. There is never any

doubt as to what the poet intends to convey. Not for Thomas was that fuzzy type of thinking and expression where only God and himself knew what any particular line meant and he would have considered the senseless repetition of a phrase such as "a rose is a rose is a rose" as an abuse of the faculty of speech and the power of understanding. Thomas knew that poetry, like any other human act, must have reason for its guide. Thomas was eminently human and whether he was writing poetry or philosophy he behaved like a human being. Enthusiastic admirers of his philosophy might dub him *Divus Thomas* or *Angel of the Schools;* those who were carried away by his poetry might give him the title of song bird of the Eucharist. But Thomas, although his head might be in heaven, kept his feet firmly planted on the earth. He was always the man from Rocca Sicca whose only title to divinity was the grace of God within him.

Chapter 15

Pope's Counselor

THOMAS was not destined to stay behind his breastworks in Paris and hurl back the attacks of the Arabians. He was soon to don the crusader's armor and ride into the East to challenge the Musselman champions on their own soil. Paris had the opportunity of thrilling to his eloquent tongue during the Lent of 1259, when he preached the Lenten course in the Chapel of St. James. Immediately Lent was over, or possibly before the end of the holy season, Thomas was on his way to Valenciennes, a fortified town at the junction of the Rhondelle and Schelde Rivers, in the county of Hainout (now the department of Nord), France. There the Dominican general chapter was scheduled to be held and Thomas had been summoned thither by the Master General, St. Raymond of Penafort, on a special assignment. Here Thomas in conjunction with Albert the Great, Florentius of Gaul, Bonushomo, and Peter of Tarantasia drew up a *ratio studiorum* or curriculum of studies for the Order. This *ratio* was followed by the Dominican Order for centuries and its vestiges can be quite easily discerned in the present *ratio studiorum* of the Order. At the same chapter it was decided, at the instigation of Raymond, who was a Spaniard, to erect special schools in Spain to prepare Dominican missionaries to the infidels of the Near East.

Raymond, whose fame in history hinges principally on the fact that he was the greatest canonist of his time and the man who first codified the amorphous body of Church law, had had a singularly colorful career for a canonist. During part of his strenuous life he had labored among the Moors in Spain and the conversion of the East was close to the old man's heart. He believed that in the face of an orderly philosophical attack the faith of the Musselman in the fantastic revelations supposedly granted to the immoral, raggle-taggle camel driver who became the prophet Mohamed, would crumble. Raymond, with the enthusiastic approval of Pope Alexander IV, ordered Thomas to undertake the task. Thomas was occupied with this work until 1264, when it was without delay translated into several languages of the East. This work, the greatest of the philosophic works of Aquinas, is known as the *Summa Contra Gentiles — Summa Against the Infidels*. Therein unaided by the authority of Christian revelation and basing his arguments principally upon Aristotle, whom the Orientals considered their own, Thomas stands to the full height of his great stature as a philosopher and dialectician.

But Thomas was not occupied solely with the writing of this *Summa* between the years 1259 and 1264. He continued his teaching and preaching. Although his time as a master at the University of Paris had expired he returned thither at the insistent pleading of the university authorities. The university which a few years before had been so violently opposed to the Dominicans that it wished to drive them beyond the pale and which still cherished no great love for them now discovered that with the departure of the most illustrious professor, a member of that Order, its schools were losing their prestige and students were deserting its halls to flock to other universities. The general of the Order, anxious to accept any token that might be construed as a peace offering, sent Thomas back to Paris. There he remained until 1261.

Alexander IV died in the month of May, 1261, and he was succeeded by Jacques Pantaleon, Patriarch of Jerusalem, who mounted the throne of the Fisherman as Urban IV. The new pontiff had scarcely waited to set the tiara straight on his venerable brow before he issued a command to Thomas to leave Paris and come to Rome to be the Pope's theologian. Who had a better title than the Pope to the service of the brains of the Church? So the summer of 1261 found Thomas plodding across the Alps to Italy, his native heath.

Urban IV, like Raymond of Penafort, harbored within his breast suppressed desires. As Raymond ardently longed for the conversion of the Saracen, the ex-Patriarch of Jerusalem panted like the thirsty hart for the extinction of the Greek schism. Like Raymond, too, he believed that if he could get a first-class theologian to point out their errors to them the Greek resistance would crumble and the straying sheep would return to the fold of the Good Shepherd. Having become Pope he used his new authority *instanter* to press into service in this cause the prolific pen of Christendom's best mind. At Urban's behest, Thomas had no sooner reached Rome than he started the writing of his celebrated treatise against the errors of the Greeks — *Contra Errores Graecorum* — on which he worked from 1261 to 1264. Concurrently with this work he also wrote another allied tract *De Rationibus Fidei Contra Saracenos, Graecos et Armenos* at the request of a dignitary of the Church of Antioch who was probably an old friend of the Pope. These two works are still the best in the field. Also at the Pope's request Thomas wrote his *Catena Aurea — The Golden Chain* — a commentary on the four gospels, the first part of which, the commentary on Matthew, was written between 1261 and 1264.

In addition to these few writing chores, Thomas also labored in the pulpit in the cities in which the papal court was held — Rome, Orvieto, and Viterbo. Every year he drew the star assignment at St. Peter's, the Lenten course, which was by custom assigned to the greatest preacher in Italy. And Urban was not ungrateful. Time after time he urged Thomas to accept the cardinal's hat with rich benefices. Thomas steadfastly refused the honors with as much determination as he had rejected the abbacy of Monte Cassino to become a Dominican. In 1262 the Dominican, Richard Annibaldi de Moralia, who succeeded to Thomas' chair at the University of Paris, was summoned to Rome by Urban, probably at the request of Thomas, made Master of the Sacred Palace and Cardinal some time later.

Richard, like Thomas, was an Italian nobleman and the two had been close friends at Paris. Upon Richard's coming to Rome, this friendship was renewed and upon his elevation to the Sacred College, Thomas was a frequent visitor at the Castle of Moralia, the cardinal's family estate near Rome. The castle, as a result of a visit Thomas made there, became the setting of a dramatic incident which caused a great sensation in Rome at that time. While on a visit there on Christmas Eve, Thomas was introduced to two of Rome's leading Jewish rabbis. The conversation naturally concerned religion and Thomas, it may be presumed, held the floor a good part of the time, proving to the two learned Jews that Jesus was the Messiah promised by the Old Law and with the institution of His Church the centuries' long mission of Judaism had been fulfilled. Yet in spite of the persuasive powers and irrefutable argumentation of Aquinas, the rabbis remained in the end unconvinced. However, Thomas begged them to give mature thought to the evidence he had presented and arranged a rendezvous with them for the following day at the same place. Thomas recognized that reason had done all it could. None knew better than he that although reason may prepare the way for, it is powerless to give, Faith. God alone can grant that great gift. The soul of Faith by which a man is reborn comes, like the human soul, directly from the hands of the Creator. Thomas, upon returning to his convent, spent the entire night in prayer, imploring Christ to celebrate His birthday on the morrow by granting spiritual nativity to these two brothers of His blessed mother's blood.

On the following day when the two rabbis returned to the cardinal's castle they were received into the Faith. It might be mentioned in passing that there is nothing unusual about the fact that two prominent Jews were received as honored guests at the castle of an Italian cardinal. Although non-Catholic historians are accustomed to pass over the fact, it remains a matter of historical record that at Rome the Jews suffered little persecution and that modicum came from the people and not from the Church. This perennially persecuted people found in the Popes their stanchest protectors and in the City of the Popes their safest haven.

In addition to bringing Jews into the Church Aquinas undertook, about this time, a work that was to be of inestimable benefit to them. For it was about 1263, that he started the treatise, *De Regimine Judaeorum* at the request of the Duchess of Brabant, which was finished probably in 1267. The Duchess of Brabant, an old friend of Thomas and his family, had among her subjects a great number of Jews. And, during the middle ages, as at other times throughout the course of history, the Jews constituted a serious political problem. The people, who stigmatized them as the murderers of Jesus, regarded them with aversion and treated them with contempt. The Jews reacted by harboring toward the "Christian dogs" a less obvious but equally deep hatred. Shakespeare in his *Merchant of Venice* has drawn the picture of the situation for the ages.

Now, the Jews may have been contemned but they possessed a genius, peculiar to themselves, for making and holding on to money. In most of the medieval kingdoms the Jews owned a good share of the currency but in Brabant, in particular, they all but bled the state white. If the Jews had been treated as decent citizens, of course, they probably would have contributed their share as citizens to the up-keep of the state. But outcast as they were they kept their money and let the state struggle on as best it could. Now, of course, the medieval princes could have anticipated the practices of Hitler and forced the Jews to disgorge their riches by persecution and confiscation. But at this time there was morality in the world and any prince so doing would have felt the weight of the Church's wrath as Hitler would have felt the heavy hand of Pius XI were it not for the fact that centuries ago the Pope's strong right arm was broken and since that time it has hung limp and powerless by his side.

The Duchess of Brabant thought that the Jews should contribute to the support of the state which sheltered them. She wrote to Thomas pointing out that in her country the Jews had a corner on the wealth and to the great teacher she proposed two questions, viz. (a) would it be just to impose a heavy but proportionate tax upon the Jews? (b) would it be a breach of ruling ethics to force the Jews to wear a distinctive garb so that her tax-collectors could find them with less difficulty? To both questions Thomas replied in the affirmative with certain distinctions and restrictions. The Jews, he answered could be taxed, in proportion to their wealth, but not as Jews. They had a duty to support the state and if that duty were not met with willingly then tribute could be forced upon them. The same regarding the garb. That was to single them out, not as Jews, but as taxable citizens of the state who had the tendency to dodge their obligations. However, Thomas goes out of his way to defend the Jews' right to freedom of conscience and to point out that no penalty could be laid upon Jews as Jews. And this was a new departure from the trend of the middle ages.

Thomas stayed with Pope Urban IV as papal theologian until 1264. The times were hazardous and the troubles of the Pope many. Manfred, the son of Frederick II, continued where his father had left off in his struggle against the Papacy and during the pontificate of Urban this struggle reached its height. Manfred attacked the Papal states and besieged Rome. Urban retired to Orvieto, whence he summoned Manfred to appear under pain of censure. Manfred disregarded the threat. Urban finally appealed to the French who descended upon Italy and brought peace for a time. In the midst of all this turmoil Thomas stood like the place of his birth, a dry rock to which the Pope could flee for consolation, advice, and spiritual rejuvenation. While another of his cutthroat cousins bedeviled Mother Church the man from Rocca Sicca remained stanch by the side of the Vicar of Christ. He has remained there ever since.

Chapter 16

The Office of Corpus Christi

IT was at the command of Urban IV, the Pope responsible for so much of the work of Aquinas, that Thomas tried his hand at poetry for the first and last time of his life, when he undertook to write the office for the Feast of Corpus Christi which the Pope established in 1274. The institution of this feast was the greatest act of Urban's pontificate and his selection of Thomas as the author of the Mass and office of the feast, whether by accident or design, was an inspired choice, which resulted in the Church's obtaining for her most sublime devotion a magnificent liturgical masterpiece.

The events leading up to the institution of the Feast of Corpus Christi, which was responsible more than any other single factor before the pontificate of Pius X of keeping the faithful mindful of the true center of their devotion, the ineffable sacrament of the altar, are not directly concerned with the life of Thomas Aquinas. But they are concerned, and that most intimately, with the history of his Order in which devotion to the Holy Eucharist has always held the principal place, a place which no other devotion has ever been allowed to usurp despite the spiritual fads and fancies of seven centuries. Writers have often speculated as to whether or not Thomas would have been the great theologian he was had he not become a Dominican. It is one of those idle speculations that sometimes tempt the historian to digress from the direct pursuit of his narrative. But it is a bootless speculation because no answer to the question can be given with certainty.

But whether or not Thomas became the Church's greatest theologian as a Benedictine, a Franciscan, a Norbertine, or a Carthusian, it is probable that the title of Eucharistic Doctor would still have gone to some Dominican because of the intense emphasis with which the Order, from the beginning has stressed that devotion. And so, although Thomas is not concerned with the early history of this feast, the Order that formed and fostered his devotion to the hidden and helpless Jesus is concerned.

The story goes back to the year 1230 when Jacques Pantaleon, that son of a poor French cobbler, was Archdeacon of Liège. There he made the acquaintance of two holy ladies, Juliana of Cornillon, a Cistercian nun, and a mystic named Eva, who lived in a hermitage near the Church of St. Martin at Liège.

Juliana dwelt at the Convent of Mont Cornillon, where the sisters conducted a large hospital designed for the reception of pilgrims who returned from the Holy Land, as many did in those days, stricken with the living death of leprosy. Juliana had come to the nuns as an orphan when she was a very small child. The sisters had brought her up in the love of God and Juliana repaid them for their efforts because she became noted for the holiness of her life and especially for her all consuming love of our Lord in the Blessed Sacrament. So great was her love of the Eucharist that a special oratory was given her for her use where she could retire after receiving Holy Communion and where, in those days of infrequent reception of the sacrament, Juliana often remained for a week at a time in meditation and prayer after the great event.

In the year 1208, when Juliana was about sixteen, she had a vision while she was rapt one day in contemplation in her oratory. It seems that she beheld the moon which appeared to be at its full but she could not see the whole moon because it was disfigured by a dark blot which partly obscured it. Juliana paid no attention to the vision the first time but after it had appeared to her again and again she began to worry, so going to her superior she told what she had beheld. The superior called in learned counsel and these theologians discounted the whole tale as a case of nerves or some such derangement of the psychophysical system.

But Juliana knew that she had not dreamed or imagined what she saw and she spent long hours in prayer begging for an explanation of her vision. When she finally, worn out from her long vigil, fell into a heavy slumber an answer was given to her in sleep. In the depths of her soul, says Juliana, Christ spoke to her saying, "The vision that has disturbed thee means this: there is lacking in my Church militant a feast that I wish to have established. It is the Feast of the Most Blessed Sacrament. At present this feast is observed only on Holy Thursday and, since on that day my Passion and death are the principal things to be considered, I desire that another day be reserved on which it shall be celebrated in solemn festival by all Christendom. For this there are three reasons! That the faith in this divine mystery, which is now being attacked, and which, in the future, will be even further menaced, be confirmed and strengthened. Secondly, that the faithful who seek the truth may be more fully instructed and that these may draw from the Spring of Life the strength they need to live virtuously. Thirdly, that reparation may be made, by a sincere and profound worship of the Most Blessed Sacrament, for the irreverence and impiety shown toward the divine majesty of the sacrament of the altar." And then, Juliana was appointed to prepare for the establishment of this feast.

Juliana did not give much evidence of being the proper person for the mission because it was not until 1230, almost twenty years after she had received her assignment that she got to work on it. In that year she became prioress of her convent. Then she sought the advice of John of Lausanne, a man of great reputation for sanctity, on the subject and John presented the matter to a board of theologians composed of the Bishop of Cambray; the Chancellor of Paris; Jacques Pantaleon, Archdeacon of Liège; Hugh of St. Cher, the Dominican Provincial; and three other Dominican theologians. After a thorough examination of the reported vision the scholars decided that the revelation was at least in conformity with the spirit of the Church and that the institution of the feast would certainly do no harm to the piety of the faithful, for the love of the Blessed Sacrament, characteristic of the early Church, was gradually dying out.

The news that the institution of such a feast was contemplated caused stiff and bitter opposition — and from the clergy, a proof if one was needed that its institution was a necessity. However, feeling ran so high that it was not until 1245 that the Bishop of Liège published the order that Thursday ofter the octave of Pentecost be thenceforward reserved for the celebration of the Feast of Corpus Christi. The bishop's death prevented the execution of his decree. But the feast was observed by the Canons of St. Martin's who began in 1247 to keep it with great solemnity.

In 1252, the Dominican, Hugh of St. Cher, who in the meantime had been made cardinal and papal legate to Germany and the Low Countries, visited Liège during the time of the feast. He celebrated the Mass of the Blessed Sacrament, which had been composed by a Cistercian, and preached on the Holy Eucharist. Afterward by solemn decree, he commanded that the feast be observed by all the clergy of the dioceses of the territory to which he was Legate. Juliana was not among those present when the Dominican brought her dreams to triumphant realization. She had been hounded out of the diocese by the clergy. However, she left in her friend Eva, the hermitess, an alter ego who enjoyed her triumph for her.

And Eva did more. When Jacques Pantaleon became

Urban IV, Eva caused him to be reminded of his younger years, when as Archdeacon of Liège he first heard Juliana's story and a petition was presented by the Bishop of Liège for the establishment of the feast throughout the universal Church. But Urban was not inclined to do much about it at that time for Italy was in the throes of civil war and the Pope, himself, was an exile from Rome. Meanwhile, Aquinas, who had been in England for a short while in attendance at the Dominican general chapter of 1263, returned to Italy. The Pope summoned him to Orvieto to again offer him the cardinal's hat as a token of appreciation for the completion of the first part of the *Catena Aurea*. Thomas again refused the proffered reward. But there is an old saying and a true one that every man has his price. Thomas had his and being a truly great man his desires were anything but picayune. They soared beyond the limits of space and time as Christ, like Urban, was one day to discover when He, like Urban, asked Aquinas to name his price. For Urban to offer the cardinal's hat to Thomas was like a woman offering a smile instead of her pearls as a bribe to a two-gun bandit; like Austria offering a city or two to Adolph Hitler. Such niggardly recompense could never satisfy the rapacious Thomas. So when the Pope asked this spiritual bandit to name his price he named one far beyond the value of any hat be it cardinal red or royal purple. Thomas demanded the institution of the Feast of the Blessed Sacrament throughout the universal Church.

The Feast of Corpus Christi has been called the "Festival of St. Thomas and the Friars Preacher." This, of course, is a slight exaggeration. Yet when we consider the part played by the Dominicans in the establishment of the festival we find it contains more truth than is usually to be found in such enthusiastic generalizations. Four Dominicans were members of the eight-man board that first recommended its institution. A Dominican cardinal was the first to extend its observance beyond the confines of a single diocese. And finally it was a Dominican who secured its observance by the universal Church. In the liturgy peculiar to the Order of Preachers the feast has always held equal rank with Christmas, Easter, and Pentecost. The Pope having promised to institute the feast commissioned Thomas to write the liturgy for it.

According to Denis, the Carthusian, St. Bonaventure received a like commission but destroyed what he had written after seeing the work done by Aquinas. There is nothing definitely to disprove the story but it has all the earmarks of countless Franciscan-Dominican legends coming out of the middle ages. It is surprising how many of the wonderful happenings of early Franciscan lore are repeated in the *Vitae Fratrum* of the Dominicans with the only changes being the fact that Dominicans rather than Franciscans play the stellar roles. Far be it from us to sit in the scorner's seat and assume the cynic's sneer especially since we are unable to produce a single bit of evidence to disprove the wonder stories. But it is suggested that, when you undertake to read some of the alleged histories of these two old orders that have their roots in the dim and distant past, you be tolerant and read them in the spirit in which they were written — as true to the hero's character if not always true to fact.

They were wonderful men, those early friars. Anyone who questions that is referred to the *Opera Omnia Sancti Thomae Aquinatis*, the monumental collection of the authenticated works which Thomas wrote in twenty-five years between lectures, sermons, cross-continental hikes and, lest we forget, prayers. They were exceptionally holy men and it cannot be doubted that God showered sensible signs of His approbation upon saints like Francis, Dominic, Bonaventure, and Thomas. But some of the little tales and wonder stories enhance neither the stature of the men nor of their Orders to the modern mind. Such stories are as harmful to the early friars as the *Introduction to the Eternal Gospel* was prejudicial to the cause of the regulars, for they lessen credibility in extraordinary events that were probably genuine miracles. They hold to history the same relation that the apocryphal gospels hold to Sacred Scripture.

This story, for example, about Bonaventure destroying his manuscript, while no wonder story, is rather far-fetched. There seems to be no good reason why Urban should have given both men the assignment. Surely he realized that either man was capable of turning in a satisfactory piece of work. There is no record that the Pope opened the other chores he assigned to Thomas to the great Franciscan's competition. In this case the yarn was probably manufactured by some Dominican who was trying to carry coals to Newcastle by thus exalting the genius of Thomas. It was probably accepted without challenge by the Franciscans who were not at all annoyed at having their holy general shown as such a humble man.

But even though the story may not be true, the general idea it was meant to convey is plain. The office written by Thomas for the Feast of Corpus Christi is a masterpiece, the beauty and sublime poetical splendor of which could not have been approached by any man then living — not even Bonaventure. It has been called "an immortal masterpiece, in which poetry, piety, and faith, dispute the palm." It contains such poetical gems as the *Lauda Sion*, the *Sacris Solemniis*, the *Verbum Supernum*, the *Pange Lingua*, and that sparkling bit of prose poetry, that jubilant prayer of thanksgiving, the antiphon, *O Sacrum Convivium*.

The office and Mass as a whole constitute a complete history of the Blessed Sacrament not only as it was instituted in the New Testament but as it was foreshadowed in the Old. In addition to being a history, it is a theological compendium on the Holy Eucharist. Anyone knowing the theology contained therein knows all that he ever need know, almost all that he ever can know about the greatest sacrament. And the whole, whether in poetry or in prose, is characterized by a simplicity that is surpassed only by its beauty and related in language within the comprehension of a child.

The office opens on the historical note with the antiphon after the psalms bringing us back to the upper room in Jerusalem where our Divine Lord is preparing the altar for the first Mass. "Christ Our Lord," we are told "the eternal priest according to the order of Melchisedech took bread and wine." The historical note is continued with the capitulum which Thomas selected from the eleventh chapter of St. Paul's first epistle to the Corinthians: "The Lord Jesus on the night that he was betrayed took bread, and giving thanks, broke and said, 'Take and eat. This is my body which shall be delivered for you.'" The response to the capitulum refers to the parable in which Christ related the story of the man who had prepared a great feast and sent his servant out to round up those who had been invited. "Everything is ready," ends the response.

The opening hymn of the office, *Pange Lingua,* then begins with its wonderfully complete historico-theological conspectus of the Last Supper. This hymn has been chosen by the Church as the special paean of the Blessed Sacrament. The last two verses of it, known to Catholics throughout the world as the *Tantum Ergo,* must be sung any time the Blessed Sacrament is exposed to public worship. The hymn sung at Matins, *Sacris Solemniis,* brings us once more to the cenacle where we unite ourselves with the disciples as they receive the first Communion. This hymn closes with the soul-stirring verses which begin: "Panis angelicus fit panis hominum." And so the office continues to the end with soaring sublimity and ends on the note of thanksgiving that is the *O Sacrum Convivium.* In the opinion of Archbishop

Vaughn the hymns of Aquinas "form the household words of the Sanctuary and the very language of the Holy Place. . . . What writer has so fixed his name in every Sanctuary, or has made ten thousand churches ring for hundreds of years, with such an ever-repeated, never omitted anthem of joy and praise. . . . He, the champion of the Blessed Sacrament, as if by heavenly inspiration, poured out his numbers in a poet's prayer."

Urban IV celebrated the Feast of Corpus Christi for the first time on the Thursday following the octave of Pentecost, 1264. In August of the same year he issued a bull commanding the institution of the feast in the universal Church. The greatest act of his pontificate achieved, Urban died at Perugia, October 2, 1264, and the man from Rocca Sicca, no longer private theologian of the Pope, and still a simple friar, awaited his superior's assignment to a new post.

Chapter 17

Interlude at Bologna

AFTER the death of his friend, Urban, Thomas was assigned to teach at the Dominican studium at Naples. He intended to occupy himself, too, with a work of which he had long dreamed, an intense and critical study of the authentic text of the entire works of Aristotle. While he was a member of Urban's household, Thomas had met a Dominican named William of Moerbeke who was one of the greatest Greek scholars then living and Thomas had persuaded William to translate Aristotle into Latin. This does not mean, as some have supposed, that Thomas knew no Greek. He had studied Aristotle while he was disciple of Albert and he continued this study and made some commentary on the Stagyrite when he taught at Paris. But he was probably not expert in Greek and his progress was retarded by that fact. Now at Naples with William's expert and precise translation his work could proceed at a much faster rate. And, as a matter of fact, the major part of the commentaries of Aquinas on Aristotle date to this period in Naples. He welcomed the retreat to the cloister at Naples, also, because it would give him opportunity to bring another dream to reality, namely, the writing of his *Summa* of Theology, his book for beginners, which would revolutionize and facilitate the study of that science. He began this work in 1266.

In the meantime, the position left vacant by the death of Urban the Fourth had been filled when the sacred college,

assembled at Viterbo, chose another Frenchman, Guy Foulquois, as St. Peter's successor. Unlike Urban, Guy was the
son of no lowly tradesman but the scion of a noble house.
He came to the chair of Peter from a life in the world that
had been crammed with a variety of experience. Guy had not
been dedicated to the priesthood by fond parents; he had
selected it as a vocation rather late in life. A widower and
the father of a family, he had been a soldier and a lawyer
before he decided to become a priest. His rise had been rapid.
When the sacred college met at Perugia to choose a successor
to Urban, Guy was not among those present. He was at
Boulogne sur Mer in France. It is said that when he received
the news of his election he traveled to Perugia in all haste
to persuade the cardinals to elect someone else in his stead.
The college refused to change its decision and on February
22, 1265, he was elevated to the papacy under the title
of Clement IV.

Clement IV came to the throne in very trying times.
Before the election the cardinals had voted that the policy
of the Church should be a war to the finish against the
House of Hohenstaufen and to that end put the papacy
under the protection of Charles of Anjou, the youngest
brother of St. Louis IX of France. Clement decided to
follow this policy to the letter. He was a very determined
man and his first step upon becoming Pope was to forbid
his relatives access to the Vatican. He decided that if the
energy of the Church was to be directed in the proper
manner against her enemies the good, old pork-barrel would
have to be closed for the duration. Suitors for the hands
of his daughters were warned that they were marrying not
the daughters of the Pope but the immediate female descend-
ants of Guy Foulquois. The Pope put the Vatican on a war-
time basis and went all out for victory.

And Clement, businesslike as he was, remembered that
there was a Dominican friar named Thomas Aquinas to

whom the Holy See was deeply in debt. But unlike the easygoing, friendly Urban he did not call the creditor into conference to discuss the method of payment. Clement was a man with a mission and the little amenities he rather gruffly pushed aside. He went straight to the point and in the first month of his pontificate he issued a brief appointing Thomas to the Archbishopric of Naples and conferred upon him the revenue of the Monastery of Saint Peter for his support. This put Aquinas in difficulty. It was one thing to argue the gentle Urban out of making him a cardinal. It would most surely be another to persuade this ex-soldier to retract a papal brief. The Pope was most anxious that Aquinas accept the honor because he desired the benefit of his prestige and wise counsel. But Thomas was adamant. Clement, after seeing that Thomas actually dreaded assuming the dignity and fearing that he would be opposing the will of God in forcing him to accept it against his will, reluctantly withdrew the brief.

There is an historical conclusion concerning this period of Thomas' life which, if true, throws a great deal of light upon his character. It was about this year (1265) that Thomas accepted the task, at the request of Hugh, King of Cyprus, to write a treatise on government. Strangely enough it is the only work which he failed, of his own free will, to finish. Students of his life have wondered why he abandoned this task which should have been congenial. A search into Italian history of the period has disclosed that not long after Thomas accepted the assignment and began to write *De Regimine Principum* Hugh commenced a war against the Aquino family. Thomas abandoned the writing of his treatise at the fourth chapter of the second book. This is another angle on the humanity of Aquinas. Here is not the cold, passionless metaphysician but the very lifelike man from Rocca Sicca who resented having his brothers persecuted.

Thomas remained at Naples until 1267, when he was

appointed to the chair of theology at the University of Bologna at the request of the university. But before taking his post at the university, Thomas attended the general chapter of the Order of Preachers held in that city in 1267 and was present at the ceremonies conducted for the solemn translation of St. Dominic's body to the magnificent tomb which now contains the sacred relics. These rites were celebrated at Bologna on Whitsunday, June 5, 1267.

At Bologna Thomas achieved the same distinction that had been his at Paris. It is said that even the citizens of the town crowded his lecture hall to hear the man whose fame then filled the Christian world. Men of learning came from distant cities of Italy to sit at his feet as simple students. It must be understood that Thomas, notwithstanding the scantiness of extant biographical material on him, was not the genius of story and proverb who was obscure in his own generation. Aquinas did not have to wait for posterity to extol a talent that was ignored by his own age. Quite the contrary. His fame as a teacher received a wider recognition in his own day than it has since. He was the dominant figure of his times. Why then, it might be asked, was a man of such stature so thoroughly overlooked? How was it possible for such a vibrant personality to remain so obscure in history? One reason, most certainly, is that the members of the Order of Preachers were not given to historical or biographical writing and his brethren were the only ones in a position to know Thomas. Another reason, possibly, is that his works attracted so much attention from the first that the man behind them was forgotten and neglected. Even today the *Summa Theologica* is seldom referred to by its proper title. It is usually called "St. Thomas." His doctrine is very often also called St. Thomas. Such statements as the following are common: "This truth is clearly expressed in St. Thomas." History probably offers no parallel case of a man being so completely identified with what he has written. St. Thomas very early, possibly even in his own lifetime, became an institution rather than a personality.

There is an anecdote concerning Thomas during his stay in Bologna, that throws another illuminating side-light upon his character. This anecdote, for a change, has nothing to do with angelic visitations or extraordinary mystical phenomena. It is right down to earth — so much so, indeed, that it is somewhat remarkable that it was ever preserved. The reason for its preservation is probably the fact that it so aptly illustrates the saint's great humility. While we do not contemn the great and necessary virtue of humility, the greatest interest this anecdote has for us who are striving to obtain a picture of Thomas without the wings, the halo, and the upturned eyes, is the fact that it brings out his humanity. The story runs thus: Thomas was one day taking his customary exercise walking up and down the corridor of the cloister when he was approached by a lay brother of the community. It was shortly after his arrival at Bologna and the lay brother, it seems, had not yet been given the opportunity of meeting the famous theologian. This was nothing strange, for the Dominican convent at Bologna was a large house and it very often sheltered for a day or two friars who were passing by on some journey or other through Italy. And as the Dominicans were a foot-loose body of men, generally to be found either going or coming, the number of transients harbored at the convent at Bologna was considerable.

Now, the brother seeing the strange priest walking slowly up and down the cloister decided that he might just as well be stretching his legs to some useful purpose. And this particular brother had such a purpose ready at hand. He had business in the city and since the rule demanded that the friars travel two by two the superior had told him to ask the first friar he met to be his companion. Thomas happened to be the first and the brother, in a very businesslike way and perhaps enjoying no little his delegated authority, gave the assignment to him. Thomas accepted his charge without comment and the two started off. But he should not have undertaken the journey. An injury or infirmity from which one of his legs suffered made it almost impossible for the limb to sustain the immense weight it had to bear. Walking on it was agony and Thomas had moderately exercised it that day only to keep it limber. On his trip with the brother the bad leg slowed his progress to such an extent that the priest found it impossible to keep pace with the brother. He found himself lagging behind. The impatient brother was forced to halt several times to allow his companion to catch up with him. Whereupon he reproached the priest for his sluggishness and that in a voice that was no whisper.

Finally the pair arrived at the market place and as the brother was making his rounds, Thomas took advantage of the opportunity offered to observe the methods of the tradesmen. He noted the prices of articles for sale. He listened to indignant customers as they disputed the prices quoted. He examined the weights used on the scales. He saw the butcher, when dealing with a young or inexperienced buyer, add his own huge, red hand to the weight of a leg of mutton. He asked questions from both buyers and sellers. So, for Thomas, the afternoon was by no means a loss. He used it for a little field work in particular justice. Returning home he put aside the *Summa* or whatever else he had been engaged in writing and penned a treatise on buying and selling, the well-known opusculum, *De Emptione et Venditione*.

In the meantime, the poor brother had learned the identity of the companion on whom he had rubbed the rough edge of his tongue that afternoon and he immediately hastened to the great teacher's cell to beg his pardon. The story runs that the brother threw himself at the feet of Aquinas and begged to be forgiven and so forth and so forth. Thomas was very much embarrassed and answered with his "usual sweetness." "It is not your fault, dear brother, it was mine, or rather the fault of my suffering leg, that I could not walk faster, or help you as I should wish to have done." This is an example of dialogue, put into the mouth of Thomas by one who was anything but a master of the art. Thomas, whose whole life was consecrated to truth, would not have lied to preserve his humility. The lay brother certainly was at fault in giving way to impatience and chiding the unknown priest. However, the whole story, including the dialogue, was aimed at bringing out the saint's humility which illustrates the saying about painting the lily. His obscured humanity, which is so well pointed out by the account, was not taken into account by the early biographers.

In August 1267, Thomas left Bologna and journied to Viterbo at the summons of Clement IV. The Pope decided that in the rocky seas on which the bark of Peter was being tossed, the ancient ship needed the guidance of an experienced navigator. Recalling that in the days when the bark was commanded by Urban IV, the wisdom and counsel of Thomas had proved invaluable to the captain, he decided to press that same navigator back into service. The wise course followed by Clement in his dealings with the princes may have been owing to the sage advice of this seasoned and enlightened friar. At any rate it was this task that claimed the principal attention of the man from Rocca Sicca for the greater part of the next two years.

Chapter 18

The Fall of the House of Hohenstaufen

THE House of Hohenstaufen from which Thomas was descended on the distaff side was still making a great deal of trouble for the Church. Conrad, who had succeeded his father Frederick II, was as fierce and unscrupulous but not as intelligent as his diabolic sire. It was Conrad who had visited such terrible vengeance upon the House of Aquino not long after he had taken up his father's soiled scepter. But Conrad did not live long enough to leave the imprint of his bloody hand very clearly upon history. Not long after he had sacked and killed at Rocca Sicca he met his own death at the age of twenty-seven, struck down in the flower of his youth at the beginning of a career that bade fair to rival that of his rascally father in villainy. Conrad left as heir to the throne his infant son Conradin. But since Conradin, who was but two years old, could not reign in fact, Manfred, Conrad's half-brother assumed the office of regent. Manfred was a son of whom Frederick might well have been proud. He possessed all the more revolting traits of his father's house and had he been granted a longer life might have become as great a blackguard as his father in spite of the fact that he lacked Frederick's intelligence.

Against Manfred Alexander IV and Urban IV had hurled vigorous opposition and during Urban's short reign Manfred was defeated in Lombardy by the papal troops under Guy, Bishop of Auxerre, and Robert, son of the Count of Flanders. But Manfred recuperated his military strength to such a degree that he was able to besiege Rome and drive Urban to Orvieto.

When Clement took the throne Manfred was at the height of his success. Clement continued the policy of his predecessor and much more vigorously. Urban had made advances to the French and had promised the throne of Sicily to Charles of Anjou. But Charles of Anjou was a pauper prince and was unable to secure the necessary financial backing for the prosecution of a war and in Urban's time nothing was done about it. But as soon as Clement became Pope he set about with characteristic energy supplying the impoverished Charles with the sinews of war. The position of the Holy See was precarious and Clement needed to act swiftly. He proclaimed a crusade against Manfred and sent his legates and the mendicant friars throughout Europe granting lavish indulgences to those who would support the Holy See in this crisis. It seems that there was little difficulty in obtaining men, but money was slower in coming because the clergy outside of Italy were inclined to regard the Pope's struggle with Manfred as a quarrel between two sovereigns and not a struggle between the spouse of Christ and the forces of darkness as it truly was. But Clement was a man of indomitable will and by the strength of that will and it alone he was finally able to scrape together enough money to equip an army. Charles came to Rome, by sea, just before his army marched and upon signing a treaty with the Holy See, by which he promised to respect the Church and preserve her liberty, he was solemnly crowned on January 6, 1266, at St. Peter's in Rome.

Charles lost little time in taking up the work he had been selected to do. On February 22 he scored a decisive victory over Manfred and his Saracen hordes at Benevento. In this battle Manfred was slain. Young Conradin now took over the command of the army and rallying to his banner the scattered Hohenstaufen forces advanced against Charles. He was defeated in the battle of Tagliacozzo, August 23, 1268 and he, himself, taken prisoner. Charles showed no mercy to the whelp of the wolf and had him executed in the market place at Naples on October 29. Clement IV did not long survive the last of the Hohenstaufens, the house whose power he had broken. He died at Viterbo, November 29, 1268, and was buried in the Dominican Church in that city.

So Thomas was with Clement for a little more than a year as counselor, philosopher, and friend. During this period in addition to acting as adviser to the Pope he taught at the Dominican studium in Viterbo and continued work on the *Summa*. Unlike Urban, Clement did not assign to Aquinas the writing of any controversial works. His sole purpose in calling Thomas to the papal court seems to have been the benefit of his counsel. But the fact that the Pope did not assign Thomas any particular post at the controversial front did not deter the great warrior from engaging in controversy. Since this period while he stayed at Clement's court is one during which material upon the life of Thomas is particularly scanty and since it forms, so to speak, a lull in his fighting life — because immediately after the death of Clement Thomas went to Paris where he plunged into the fiercest battle of his life — it might be well to treat here a phase of his life that we have thus far neglected, his career as a controversialist as it is demonstrated by the *Questiones Disputatae* or as we would say in English *Controversies*.

We promised at the beginning of this work to reveal to our readers a man who was, by no means, the peaceful, placid citizen they had always imagined him to be. We promised to show them a Thomas who was not only the son of a warlike house but a valiant warrior himself. Thus far only a part of this promise has been kept. We have recounted the battles Thomas waged on behalf of his Church as they appeared chronologically in his life, battles that were waged and won over a fixed period of years. But there was one fight that he waged, in season and out of season, throughout his life that could not be so circumscribed for that war did not end until after his death. The war is marked by a long series of battles covering almost twenty years and the record of those battles are known today as the *Questiones Disputatae*.

With the exception of the *Summa* there is no work of Thomas that is a more universal favorite among Thomists than the *Questiones Disputatae* for in them the great warrior is at his scintillating best. In them Aquinas defends his doctrine before the world. Scholastic debates were a regular exercise of the universities of the middle ages. Usually they were a cut and dried formality with the master setting forth his thesis and answering stock objections or questions on the subject. But when Thomas started teaching his new learning at Paris all the stilted formality was soon set aside. His classes became veritable dog fights with other masters attending his lectures for the purpose of challenging his doctrine. Much the same situation occurred in other cities — Bologna, Viterbo, Rome, and Orvieto where Thomas taught. These debates in defense of his doctrine Thomas began, according to Mandonnet's careful calculations, immediately he started teaching in Paris in 1256. During his whole time at Paris from 1256–1259 Aquinas debated on the question of truth — *De Veritate* — which forms the first of the seven questions of the work *Questiones Disputatae*. In these three years Thomas debated on the question of Truth two hundred and fifty-three times which means that twice a week, during the scholastic year which began on September 1 and ended June 29, Thomas publicly defended his teaching upon this fundamental question of philosophy. In Italy while he was traveling around with the papal court he defended the question *De Potentia* and *De Malo* — *On Evil*.

During the year Thomas spent with Clement IV at Viterbo he defended in public debate his teaching on the philosophical possibility of the Divinity uniting with human nature in the person of Christ. The tracts *De Unione Verbi Incarnati* of the *Questiones* are the result of these public disputes. Mandonnet dates these debates as taking place during the three months of September, October, and November of 1268. During the previous year from September to June he participated in further discussions on the nature of evil. Shortly after the death of Clement in November, 1268, Thomas returned to Paris where he was to match himself against the wiliest and most implacable enemy of his fighting life — the champion of Arabian philosophy, Siger of Brabant. But Siger was not to be his only opponent, for the secular professors had again become troublesome and were once more openly attacking the Orders. And in addition to these major disputes the Franciscans were waging a war of their own against the Aristotelian teaching of the Dominicans. The man from Rocca Sicca would not find Paris dull for want of action.

Chapter 19

Cannon to Right — Cannon to Left

THERE was a twofold reason why Thomas and his ever-faithful companion, Reginald of Piperno, headed for Paris at the end of the year 1268. The primary object of the trip seems to have been to fill one of the Dominican chairs at the university which had been recently left vacant by the sudden illness of the friar who occupied it. The second object was to attend the Dominican General Chapter, about to be held there, as representative of the Roman province. At the conclusion of the chapter Thomas, at the insistence of St. Louis, was permanently assigned to the chair which he had been filling as a substitute. So at the close of the Chapter, which was held during the month of May, 1269, Thomas did not return to Italy as had originally been planned.

The Dominican superiors were probably not too loathe to leave their ablest man in Paris because troubles had arisen there that demanded his presence. The agitation of the secular faculty against the Dominicans had been going on for some time. William of St. Amour had again appeared on the scene and the bitterness at the University of Paris, which had long been smouldering burst once more into flame. This time William seems to have been content to remain somewhat in the background and confine his talents to fanning the flames. His former attempt at polemical writing had been such a failure that he decided to leave the pamphleteering to someone else. The seculars soon produced a new polemicist in the person of one Gerad of Abbeville who among other things wrote as his chief attack an opus entitled *Contra Adversarium Perfectionis Christianiae — Against the Enemy of Christian Perfection* — which was merely a rehash of St. Amour's condemned work. Shortly after his arrival in Paris Thomas penned his tract *De Perfectione Vitae Spiritualis — On the Perfection of the Spiritual Life* — as an answer. The presence of Thomas in Paris and the fear he inspired with his reputation as the friend of three Popes may have caused a temporary lull in the dispute. But it did not die entirely until after the death of Thomas.

The principal struggle that engaged the attention and talents of Aquinas in Paris this time was the teaching of the Averöists led by Siger of Brabant. Concerning the seriousness of this strife the famous French philosopher, Jacques Maritain, states that it cannot be exaggerated. Siger of Brabant, whom he terms "a bold and captivating intellect," bade fair to discredit the cause of the true Aristotle by his energetic propagation of the false. M. Maritain underestimates Siger's genius. With the exception of St. Thomas he was probably the greatest dialectician then alive and possessed of an unusually keen and penetrating mind. He was the spiritual heir of Peter Abelard but in Thomas he met a greater theologian, by far, than Bernard. This time all of the odds were on the side of orthodoxy but that was not the case in the Bernard-Abelard tussle. Bernard apologized for his want of skill in dialectic by his dramatic quotation from the Fourth Book of Kings. Bernard applied to Abelard the words David spoke of the stupendous Goliath: "I am but a boy. This man has been a warrior from his youth." But in matching his strength against Thomas Siger was riding against the white knight of Christendom, a champion whose pennant had never been lowered in defeat.

There is very little known of the life of Siger of Brabant. He was a master of arts for ten years at the University of Paris and the guiding spirit of the Averöists who caused so much trouble there during the sixth and seventh decades of the thirteenth century. During the first years of the sixth decade he had the rector of the university pretty much under his thumb and Siger was the dominant figure at Paris. He was, like Thomas, a prolific writer and a persuasive speaker. Much of his works seem to have been lost, but those still existing show how dangerous was this brilliant disciple of the Arabians. *De Anima Intellectiva — On the Intellectual Soul — De Aeternitate Mundi, Questiones Naturales, Questiones Logicales* form the cleverest defense of Arabian philosophy from the pen of a European writer. His philosophy was irrational and un-Christian, but Siger's dialectic skill gave his doctrine the aura of truth. Siger, like the good Averöist he was, held that there exists but one intellect for all men. This intellect is separated from our bodies but is temporarily united to them to make thinking possible. It therefore follows that man is mortal but the race is immortal, since only the one soul exists there can be no individual immortality. Another corollary of this insidious doctrine is the absolute absence of moral responsibility. Siger's cosmology was no less dangerous. The world, he taught, was produced by a series of intermediary agencies. Therefore there is no need for Divine providence to govern men and the universe. The world itself was not created. It is coeternal with God. The only ruling force exercised upon the world comes from the conjunction of the heavenly bodies — the planets. These rule not only the world but man, the lord of the world.

But to Siger man was no "lord of the world" because the word "lord" signifies some domination. And in the philosophy of Siger man dominates nothing not even himself. For man is completely under the control of the planets as is everything else in the world. His acts are not free, therefore, but determined. Notwithstanding these heretical teachings Siger professed himself to be a true Catholic and justified the opposition existing between his faith and his philosophy by falling back on the old excuse, used frequently in the middle ages and used to some extent by the Modernist heretics, that a thing may be false in philosophy and true in religion and vice versa.

Almost as soon as he arrived in Paris Thomas rolled up his sleeves and went out after Siger. Thomas was extremely annoyed, not because Siger was a clever defender of Arabian doctrines, but because of the strong hold Averöism had obtained on the student body of the university in his absence. He was angry because the clever Averöist was forcing his sophism upon the undeveloped minds of the young. We can imagine what his attitude would be were he alive today to see the clap-trap of Siger of Brabant still being ladled out from professorial chairs at our modern universities, the old and stale materialistic stew still being offered to the young in lieu of solid food.

Thomas canceled his debates on the question *De Verbo Incarnato,* upon which he had been lecturing when he left Viterbo and which according to the custom of those days he should have continued in Paris, and set forth to meet this menace to faith and reason. He challenged Siger to a series of public debates but Siger evidently had no desire to meet the champion, for the outburst to which we referred earlier in this book was provoked from Thomas. In the treatise *De Unitate Intellectus Contra Averöistas,* which Thomas wrote, in 1270, as the culmination of his drive against Siger, he blasted Siger in words which, coming from Aquinas, are as shocking as the speech of a sailor's parrot. "If anyone," shouts Thomas, "laboring under the delusion that the clap-trap he hands out is real science, wishes to dispute anything I have written, let him oppose this treatise if he dare. And oppose it publicly not by speaking in corners or by refuting it before youngsters who are not mature enough mentally to be judges in questions of this kind. If he wishes opponents hē will be able to find plenty, and not only myself (who am the weakest of the lot) but a host of others who love truth and who will be only too willing to refute his errors and instruct his ignorance."

Concurrently with his attack on the Averöists Thomas had to fight a rear guard action upon himself and the Aristotelian doctrine he taught. This attack came from the old school theologians who regarded the rationalism of Aristotle as dangerous. These good men believed that mixing reason and Faith was dangerous business that was bound to result in great harm to, if not the destruction of, Faith. This party which was composed of practically all of the professors of theology at the university, both secular and Franciscan called themselves "the Augustinian school" and they were backed by Stephen Tempier, the Bishop of Paris and former chancellor of the university, who hated Aristotle and strongly disliked the Dominicans. In reply to the attacks of their groups Thomas wrote his *De Aeternitate Mundi — On the Eternity of the World* — and he defended his thesis in a solemn public disputation during the Lent of 1270 when he was opposed by Friar John Peckham, regent of studies for the Franciscans.

Thomas' situation seemed desperate. He was waging a frontal attack against Siger and his cohorts, he himself was being attacked by the conservatives, the Bishop of Paris was praying for a chance to condemn his teaching — and in this crisis his own brethren deserted him. A good part of the Dominicans stationed at Paris not only deserted him but joined in the battle against him. Thomas was once more on the spot with enemies closing in from all sides for the kill. Thomas did not mind fighting one or a dozen foes at the same time but he was deeply hurt by the desertion of his own brethren and by the fact that they and the Franciscans stubbornly adhered to the old, authoritative system which shied at reason. He could not seem to understand how they could be so intransigent. Could they not see that reason would not remain chained? God had made it a searching, curious, restless faculty. If they continued to deny it the activity natural to it some it would burst its bounds and turn, with murderous intent, upon its captors. For many years now its restless strivings were shown in the extravagant philosophies and heresies imported from the East and drawing thousands away from the Faith of Christ. *Augustinus dicit, Gregorious dicit, Ambrosius dicit* — this hypnotic chant could not forever keep reason in a trance. The spell would one day wear off.

But the "Augustinian school" turned its head away from Thomas. Used to looking for contradiction between the things of Faith and the things of reason they charged that the Aristotelianism of Thomas was such a contradiction. It was opposed to revealed truth, they said, therefore it was false. Thomas argued the question with them at great length with a patience such as only he possessed. Finally their stubborn irrational attitude seems to have irked him. In his tract *De Aeternitate Mundi* he drops a rather caustic comment in reference to these stiff-necked opponents: "Those who can find contradictions here," he writes, "must have more subtle minds than I: but, after all, are they not the only real wise men?"

Stephen Tempier finally got his chance to discredit Thomas. Tempier called the Averöists, Siger of Brabant and one of his followers Boethius of Daca before him to defend their teaching from charges of heresy. He commanded Thomas to present himself with these foes of his before the inquisition to defend his own teaching. This citation for Thomas to appear at the inquisitorial court was the "swing" referred to. Tempier probably already knew enough about the teaching of Aquinas to realize that he could not condemn it. He also realized that, for the greater part of the previous ten years he had spent in Italy, Thomas had been theologian of the papal curia. Tempier knew that should he dare condemn Aquinas out of spite the Pope would certainly not be pleased with him for thus casting aspersions upon papal orthodoxy. So it would appear that the summons given Thomas was given out of spite and for the purpose of discrediting him at Paris.

Thomas, of course, easily cleared himself. Siger of Brabant and his follower were condemned. But the condemnation did not stop Siger. He continued to propagate his teachings. However, his rule over the minds of men had been effectively broken, and not by Tempier but by Aquinas. Siger was again condemned in 1277 by the grand inquisitor of France. He went to Rome to appeal the decision and while in Italy he was murdered by his secretary.

Undisturbed by the spite of the Bishop of Paris Aquinas continued his writing, lecturing, and debating. He was nearing the end of the second part of the great work of which he dreamed, the *Summa Theologica,* which would revolutionize the teaching of theology. The *Questiones Disputatae* produced during this period prove that Tempier's spiteful gesture did not keep Thomas out of the public eye. His work against the Averöists, *De Anima,* was already finished so for the next two years he turned his attention to the "Augustinian school." Between 1270 and 1272 he completed *De Virtutibus in Commune — On the Virtues in General —* and in addition to this broad study of the virtues he found time to discuss particular virtues, for *De Caritate — On Charity,* and *De Correctione Fraterna, On Fraternal Correction* as well as *De Spe, On Hope* and *De Virtutibus Cardinalibus, On Cardinal Virtues,* are also products of these two years. He likewise continued his commentaries on Aristotle and research scholars date several of his greatest works to these two years. *Perhermenias, Metaphysics, De Coelo et Mundo, De Meteorologica, De Generatione —* all date from these last years at Paris. In addition to these about six of the opuscula were written in these crowded years.

All in all during his two years in Paris the man from Rocca Sicca managed to keep busy but not out of trouble. But his time at Paris came to an end in 1272. Shortly after Easter of that year Thomas left the city that had witnessed his greatest triumphs. Paris was never again to see her most brilliant son for this time when Thomas and his companion, Reginald of Piperno, left the gates of the old city behind they were not walking as heretofore. Too much work and too little sleep had sapped the strength from the great body of Aquinas and his legs were not strong enough to carry the giant from across the Alps to his native land. So this time Thomas and Reginald went through the gates mounted on donkeys. It must have been a sight to see — the huge Thomas on a donkey. Don Quixote on Rosinante could not compare, in drollness, to the man from Rocca Sicca astride an ass, which probably never in its life put in a harder day's work than it did during the period it carried Thomas to Italy. However, chances are that it did not have to do all the work. It would be characteristic of Thomas, who classed unkind treatment of animals as a sin, that he would divide the labor of bearing him between both animals. So it is the cool of the morning, the long road stretches ahead and — beyond the Alps lies Italy.

Chapter 20

Last Labors

WHILE Thomas had been battling in Paris the Holy See had been having troubles of its own. After the death of Clement IV the Church was without a head for two years and ten months. The Sacred College could not agree on a candidate. Some of the cardinals thought that two Frenchmen in succession were quite enough for the time being and they held out for an Italian and one who would be favorable to the Empire. The others did not wish to run the risk of putting the Church back at the mercy of the emperors and they favored the election of a non-Italian, preferably a Frenchman, since Charles of Anjou had assumed the protection of the Holy See. Despite the pleas that came from all quarters for a speedy election the conclave dragged on. The new King of France, Philip the Bold, and his uncle, Charles of Anjou, King of Sicily made a special visit to the conclave at Viterbo on March 10, 1271, to urge the cardinals to fill the vacancy at the head of the Church for the good of Christendom. The cardinals were deaf to this plea as they had been to all others. They were in no mood for compromise.

One of the cardinals, the Englishman John Tolet, humorously suggested that the roof of the papal palace, the site of the conclave, should be removed so that the Holy Ghost could have free access. Whether or not they were acting on this advice cannot be determined, but the people of Viterbo actually did uncover the roof. They also threatened to cut off the food supply of the cardinals unless the matter was brought to a speedy close. The roof was replaced and the embargo lifted when the cardinals threatened to put the city under interdict and to excommunicate the city fathers. Finally the cardinals, owing to the incessant urging of St. Bonaventure, did decide to come to a compromise and on September 1, 1271, they appointed a committee to elect the new Pope. This committee of six cardinals soon made an end to the matter and chose Theobald Visconti, archdeacon of Liège, an Italian who had long lived in France, to be the successor of St. Peter. He mounted the throne under the title of Gregory X.

Theobald, the son of the noble house of the Visconti of Piacenza, had been born in the year 1210 and was educated for the Church from early youth. He was a brilliant student and his rise in the Church was rapid. In 1242 he refused the bishopric of his native Piacenza and in 1245 we find him a student at the University of Paris where he remained until 1265, not as a student all of the time, but because St. Louis became attached to him. When St. Louis was preparing to go on his last crusade Theobald determined to go too. Had he not been dissuaded he might have met death with the king at Tunis in 1270. He became instead archdeacon of Liège and held that position until he was elected to the papacy in 1272.

Gregory lost no time in starting things moving. Four days after his coronation, which occurred on March 27, 1272, he issued an encyclical to inform Christendom that a General Council was to be held, beginning May 1, 1274, for the purpose of uniting the separated Greeks with Rome. This was the Council of Lyons which figures in the life of Thomas Aquinas. Shortly afterward he increased the membership of the Sacred College adding to its number six of the most illustrious men then living, including St. Bonaventure and the famous Dominican theologian, Peter of Tarantasia, and he appointed Thomas d'Agni di Lentina, the man who had received Thomas into the Order, Patriarch of Jerusalem.

There is an amusing anecdote connected with Bonaventure's appointment to the Sacred College. At the time of his appointment Bonaventure was at the small convent of Migel near Florence. When the legates from the Pope arrived bringing with them the cardinal's hat they found Bonaventure sitting under a tree washing the dinner dishes. When they proffered him the cardinal's hat, the symbol of his new office, Bonaventure pointed to a low-hanging branch and directed them to put the hat there while he finished the dishes.

Early in his pontificate Gregory also announced that it was his intention to regain control of the Holy Land and that he would bend all his energy to this end. But he realized that to perform this task a united Europe was necessary, so the Pope spent the first two years of his reign in promoting peace throughout Christendom. In order to conciliate the the Ghibelline cities of Lombardy he restored to them the ecclesiastical privileges, of which they had been deprived by his predecessors for supporting the House of Hohenstaufen. Much of the work of conciliation in the north was entrusted to the Dominican John of Viterbo. Gregory's agent, in pacifying the Guelf cities and bringing them to support the new papal attitude to the Ghibellines, was the Dominican Master-general, John of Vercelli. The Pope was making heroic efforts to bring peace to Italy and the world.

In the meantime Thomas had been busy, as usual, about his Father's business. Upon his arrival in Italy in the early June of 1272 he went immediately to Florence where he attended the Dominican chapter being held in that city, which was the main reason why he had left Paris. With him to the chapter he carried an appeal from the Paris Dominicans for his return thither. But the capitular fathers had other plans for Thomas. The appearance of the second part of the *Summa* had shown the world at large the depths of his genius and various universities had appealed to the superiors

of the Order for his services. The two most favored by the
Dominicans to benefit by the learning of Aquinas were Rome
and Naples. The fact that Charles of Anjou was so insistent
in his appeals won the favor for Naples.

The time between the close of the General Chapter in
June and the beginning of the scholastic year at Naples in
October Thomas seems to have spent in Rome in the
Dominican Convent of Santa Sabina. The old house must
have held memories for him since it was here that he first
came when fleeing Naples and the wrath of Theodora. It was
here that he had refused to see his mother and so great was
the lament she made that it became necessary for the superiors
to spirit Thomas out of the city. But at Santa Sabina Thomas
had more than memories to occupy his attention. His great
work, the *Summa* was only partly finished. The third and
last part *De Christo* now took the greater part of his time.
It may be, too, that some of the great, poetic prayers such
as the famous *Gratias ago,* recited by many priests after the
celebration of Mass was written at this time. There are about
nine such prayers attributed to Thomas and they all bear
the stamp of his genius but scholars have never been able to
fix the date of their composition. Otherwise he seems to have
given all his time to the *Summa.* If that is the case these
two months are the most inactive in the life of Aquinas. However it is very probable that he was taking an enforced rest
by the orders of his superiors because of his failing health.

At any rate the stop at Rome did not last long. Thomas
was on the road again before August because it is a matter
of record that he was present at the death of his brother-in-
law, Roger dell Aquilla, Count of Traetta. But before leaving
Rome he suffered an attack of fever at the palace of Richard
Cardinal Annibaldi. Reginald also became ill. Thomas soon
recovered his health but Reginald was given up by the
physicians. Thomas visited his faithful friend and cured him
with a relic of St. Agnes which he always carried.

Upon his arrival at Naples to take up his duties as professor at the university he was given a great reception. A local boy who had made good was returning to the folks back home and the town was not slow to show its appreciation. The ovation given this renowned son of the Aquinos was one of the greatest and most enthusiastic that the city had ever witnessed. An American is inclined to suspect the historians, who report the event, of drawing the long bow in the recognized medieval fashion. But one acquainted with the Italians and the Italian mind finds nothing untoward in the tale. Famous artists, scholars, and preachers could always draw a more spontaneous acclaim from the Italians than conquering heroes and even today St. Rocco gets a bigger crowd in his parade than the local politico.

Thomas was met at the gates of the city by a delegation of the nobles of Church and state and escorted to the famous Convent of St. Dominic through streets jammed with people who were anxious to see this son of their most noble house who had won the world's acclaim for his holiness and learning. Arrived at the convent he was not allowed to retire to his prayers and studies as he desired. The cardinal legate of Sicily wanted to speak with the great theologian. So he persuaded the archbishop of Capua who had studied under Thomas to go with him to the Dominican convent. It is said that Thomas had already become engaged on some problem and that when he came down to the parlor it was still on his mind. Entering the room where his distinguished visitors were awaiting him, Thomas, completely absorbed, did not even notice them. After standing for a time wrapped in thought his face brightened and he exclaimed aloud, "Ah, I have found what I wanted." The cardinal who had never before met Thomas did not know what to think of this strange reception but the archbishop, who knew that such abstractions were not unusual with Thomas, begged the prince of the Church to be patient. After a while the cardinal attracted Thomas' attention by the simple expedient of pulling at his sleeve and the saint came to. He was all apology for having neglected to salute his notable visitors and he proceeded, say the biographers, to talk with such delightful charm that the cardinal himself soon forgot time and space.

Thomas stayed at Naples for a year and a half. During that time he finished all that he was going to write of the third part of the *Summa* and in addition he wrote several of the opuscula. There is a very definite falling off of his work during this period. He wrote less than at any other similar period during his life. He seems to have given up public controversy, for scholars date none of the *Questiones Disputatae* after 1272. His opuscula are scanty and none of them are controversial. It seems probable that he preached little. What was the reason? It could not be old age for Thomas came to Naples when he was about forty-eight years old, just approaching that time of life when Plato says a man becomes fit to be a philosopher. It might possibly have been because of poor health. The answer to the question seems to be that he spent much more time in contemplation. It seems very likely that he could find so little time to write about God because he spent so much time looking at Him. It cannot be questioned but that Aquinas was one of the great mystics of all time. In his earlier years he had received grace to the extent that he could scientifically examine the Divinity without being carried to the peak of infused contemplation — ecstasy — so often as to seriously impede his work. He was a man with a mission and no one realized the importance of that mission more than he. It was necessary for the general good of the Church that he work constantly and prodigiously. And notwithstanding the reports of the earlier biographers that much of Thomas' work was done in ecstacy his writings do not bear the ecstatic rapture of one in a mystical trance. They are the works of a man who was very much in this world and using natural reason rather than mystical vision.

But in the last three years of his life it would seem that Thomas, in spite of himself, was carried away to ecstatic union with God more and ever more often. It is not hard to picture the saint sitting down to write about God only to be aroused perhaps hours later with the foolscap still innocent of ink. Then came the day when he laid aside his quill never again to pick it up. That day was the Feast of St. Nicholas, December 6, 1273, a little over a year after he had arrived at Naples.

Thomas had just finished his tract on the Holy Eucharist in the third part of the *Summa*. It is said that he prayed incessantly and penanced himself severely during the composition of this tract that he might be preserved from doctrinal error and also for the assurance from God on this point. As he was praying in the chapel of St. Nicholas just before the Matins of that saint were to be sung in choir, one of his colleagues, Dominic of Caserta, the sacristan of the convent and a man of sober judgment, testified that he saw Thomas raised into the air. Brother Dominic was glued to the floor. He had often heard of things like this but had never witnessed the like before. With sagging jaw, Brother Dominic watched the proceedings hardly breathing. Then from the mouth of the image of Jesus Christ on the crucifix he heard these words: *Bene scripsisti de me, Thoma. Quam ergo mercedem accipies.* "Thou hast written well of me, Thomas, what wouldst thou claim as a reward." And then, in clear tones, Dominic heard the voice of Thomas answering: *Nil nisi te, Domine.* "Only Thyself, O Lord." This is one report that has been subjected to critical scrutiny. The event has always been accepted by that most severe judge, the Catholic Church, as most probably authentic. It has been mentioned more than twenty times in papal bulls and the altar where it occurred has been enriched, by Pius V, with indulgences. The apparition on the Feast of St. Nicholas marks the climax in the life of Thomas. All that occurs after that date is the story of a different man. The Thomas we have been following is gone; the Thomas we follow henceforth is a new character. For after the kiss of Christ the man from Rocca Sicca lived only for death.

Chapter 21

The Highroad to Heaven

AFTER the Feast of St. Nicholas Reginald tried his best to persuade Thomas to finish the *Summa* at least but all of his efforts were to no avail. Thomas always answered that after what he had seen his puny work was as so much straw. In fact, so great was his disgust at the feeble attempts of reason to plumb the abyss of the Divinity that he was all for destroying the work he had done. It is said that he made several attempts to burn the *Summa* and his other theological writings. The reaction seems to be perfectly normal for even St. Paul, for all his great literary powers, confessed himself powerless to clothe in words the splendor of the Godhead. Most of us have had, in a small measure, somewhat the same experience. Any mature man who has had the opportunity of reading some heroic effort he made at composition when he was a child in the third or fourth grade has known, to a small degree, the feeling of Thomas toward his great theological works after the Feast of St. Nicholas. The composition of that tongue-chewing schoolboy may have taken the prize. The successful scholar may have been lauded by his parents and his teacher. In his mind's eye he may have seen himself a second Shakespeare. But the grown man reading the blue-ribbon theme is forced to smile and wonders if it is possible that his mind could ever have been so immature. Thomas had witnessed the vision of the Godhead. He had at last received the answer to the question of the tot at Monte Cassino, the answer which he had sought ever since to the

query: What is God? His writing on the subject seemed to
him the immature scribbling of a retarded child — just so
much straw.

In spite of anything Reginald could say Thomas refused
to write or dictate and spent most of his time in prayer.
Reginald feared that overwork had affected his mind and
asked the superiors to give Thomas a leave of absence to
regain his strength. This was granted and Reginald took
Thomas on a visit to his sister Theodora, Countess of
Marisco, whom Thomas loved most dearly. The trip was a
difficult one for Reginald because his companion fell into
ecstacy on the way. Upon his arrival at the castle the
countess greeted her beloved brother with the joy that a call
from him always evoked. But the joy soon gave way to
apprehension when Thomas failed to recognize her. "What
has happened to my brother," she asked Reginald, "that he
does not know me?" "Since the Feast of St. Nicholas," the
Dominican replied, "he has frequently been in such a state
of abstraction but I have never seen him so completely
absorbed as now." After the lapse of an hour or two Reginald
succeeded in rousing his friend. Thomas gave a deep sigh
as if waking from a restful sleep and according to Reginald
addressed him thusly: "Reginald, my son, I adjure thee by
the Omnipotent and living God, by the vows of thy order
and thy affection for me not to reveal during my lifetime
what I am about to say. The end of my labors has come.
All that I have written appears to me as so much straw,
after the things that I have witnessed and that have been
revealed to me. For the rest I hope in the mercy of God that
the end of my life may soon follow the end of my labors."

Yet in his conversation with his sister after he regained
his senses Thomas was perfectly lucid. A scrap of this
conversation has been recorded. Theodora asked her brother
how she could become a saint and Thomas had given her
the perfect answer. "Will it," he advised her. In answer to

her question, "What is the most desirable thing in life?" Thomas again gave a pithy and perfect answer: "A good death." Thomas stayed with his sister a short time and then returned to Naples. Shortly after his return he was stricken with a fever that forced him to take to his bed. He was still suffering from his illness when he received a summons from the Pope to attend the general council about to be held at Lyons. Despite his feeble health Thomas determined to answer the Pope's summons and although the whole convent knew that he was not strong enough to make the trip no one seems to have been able to stop him. An order from the Vicar of Christ superseded all authority of the Dominican superiors and the only way the Prior could have prevented Thomas from going was by an order that he was unable to give. Thomas left Naples in January on the road that was to lead not to Lyons but to Heaven.

Before he left the city his cousin, Charles of Anjou, tried to persuade him to speak well of the rule he had given Naples. Thomas told the king that he would tell the truth about Charles — nothing more or less. This determination on the part of the saint did not help set the king at ease for the truth would do Charles little good. Neither in his rule nor in his private life was Charles the type of king one would expect the brother of St. Louis of France to be, and Thomas had not been too much out of the world during his stay at Naples to know what was going on, particularly in government which he rated as one of the highest vocations given to man. So on the departure of Thomas and Reginald, January 28, 1274, they left two uneasy groups behind them — the Dominicans who were afraid that he would never reach Lyons and the king and his henchmen who were afraid that he would.

Upon leaving Naples the travelers passed through Teano on the outskirts of which town Thomas met with an accident. A tree, which had been shattered by lightning had broken and fallen across the road, forming a kind of an arch. Since there was room to pass under it nobody had bothered to remove it. The people of the happy-go-lucky middle ages would never think of doing today what could possibly, without imminent and evident catastrophe, be put off till tomorrow. Thomas, riding along on his donkey, very likely half in a trance, didn't notice the tree and for once the ever vigilant Reginald was caught napping. So in passing under the arch Thomas, sitting straight-up was hit in the head and knocked unconscious. Reginald at once went for help and came back with the dean of Teano and his nephew, a priest of the town and between the three of them they revived the fallen giant. Thomas, upon regaining consciousness protested that he had not been hurt and insisted upon continuing the journey.

The next town noted on the itinerary is Campagna on the outskirts of which was the Castle of Magenza whose mistress was Francesca d'Aquino, a niece of Thomas, who was married to the Count Annibaldi of Cecano. Here Thomas stopped to pay his respects to his relatives. He had intended to stay only a short time, perhaps overnight, but became so ill that he was forced to prolong the visit. He received the best of care at the hands of his devoted niece but in spite of everything his condition grew worse. He could not eat and even the sight of food disgusted him. The physician of the castle, one John di Guido, subjected him to all the so-called remedies within the knowledge of the medieval physician but with no result. His appetite for food did not return. Finally upon being pressed by his niece to name any food, regardless of the cost, that he felt he might be able to eat Thomas admitted that he thought he might relish a kind of fish, called herring, that he used to eat when he lived in France. The only difficulty about the request seems to be that herring were not to be had in southern Italy.

However, the leech was finally sent out on what he considered a fool's errand to obtain a few herring. At the gate of the castle he met a peasant from the estates of the castle, one Bordinaro, who was carrying a basket of sardines. Di Guido asked the man to look through his catch to see if by some chance, a herring or two got mixed up with the sardines by mistake. Bordinaro did as directed and, sure enough, under the sardines in the basket he found a number of fresh herring. John di Guido returned to the castle in triumph and proclaimed to all and sundry that a miracle had been performed, an opinion in which Father Peter di Castro, a Cistercian monk who tells the story, heartily joined. Father Peter, who had come over from the near-by monastery of Fossa Nuova with the Abbot and some other monks to see the great theologian, goes on to say that Thomas not only ate one of the fish but that his appetite was restored to him.

Thomas left the castle five days later claiming that he was now well able to travel and he and Reginald were accompanied by the Cistercians. But they had not proceeded far when Aquinas again became very ill, so ill in fact that it was out of the question to continue the journey. The monastery of Fossa Nuova was near at hand but the castle of Magenza was not far away. Thomas could have been carried without much difficulty to either. Thomas, feeling that this time he would not rise from his sickbed chose the abbey. "If Our Lord is about to visit me," he told his companions, "it is better that he should find me in a monastery than among seculars."

The monastery of Fossa Nuova to which Thomas was carried in his last illness had often sheltered members of his family long ere this. The Counts of Aquino in their days of prosperity had been patrons of this abbey as they had been of Monte Cassino. Situated in the diocese of Terracina about five miles from Magenza it was built upon the ruins of the old Roman city of Forum Appii which had been a Christian stronghold from the time the gospel was introduced into

Italy. St. Paul was welcomed to Italy by a delegation of Christians from that city upon his first voyage to Rome. Upon his arrival at the monastery Thomas insisted upon paying a visit to the Blessed Sacrament before taking to bed. As they left the chapel Thomas remarked to his faithful friend, "Reginald, my son, here is to be my last place of rest."

The great Dominican who had once rejected the opportunity of becoming a Benedictine abbot was now given the abbot's room. Once he had taken to bed the sickness that he had been fighting ever since leaving Naples took him into its grip and it became evident to all that Thomas was on his deathbed. The monks vied with one another to serve him. It is said that they themselves went to the forest to cut wood for his fire and as an act of homage to a saint carried the firewood back on their own shoulders instead of packing it on an ass. To us of the twentieth century such actions may seem a trifle foolish but little symbolic rites such as this carried a great deal of weight with the folks of the middle ages. They did not view the world and everything in it with the utilitarian's eye. A waterfall could be measured by other standards than its potential kilowatt hour production and a rainbow on a pool did not start them drilling for oil. A song was a cry escaping spontaneously from the heart not a senseless tangle of words set to a barbaric jumble of music by neurotic hack writers. That is why they were happier in spite of the fact that life was rougher and more painful and sanitary measures almost unheard of.

Thomas, it is reported, was deeply touched by this action of the monks and he chided them for thus humiliating themselves. "Whence is this," he asked, "that servants of God thus serve a man like me and bring from afar such heavy burdens?" But the monks paid him no heed and insisted upon continuing their self-imposed service. When the news that the great doctor was sick got abroad the abbey was crowded with the people of the district both gentry and peasants. From Naples and Rome came Dominican friars who had been informed of their confrère's dangerous condition.

Thomas remained thus for a month. During the entire period his mind never lost its lucidity in spite of the weakness of the body. Those by his bedside marveled at the patience with which he bore his suffering and the gentleness and charity with which he treated all who attended or visited him. Those who were frequently at his bedside during this last illness testified that he repeated over and over again a passage from St. Augustine: "So long as in me there is aught which is not wholly thine, O God, suffering and sorrow will be my lot; but when I shall be thine alone, then shall I be filled with thee, and then set wholly free."

It is rather appropriate that Thomas should have died teaching for teaching had been his life. The Thomas who had laid his pen aside in despair after the vision on the Feast of St. Nicholas was a different Thomas from the one we knew at Paris, Rome, Perugia, Bologna, and Viterbo. Now at the request of the monks he once more assumed the role to which he had been so long accustomed. The monks had set for the dying man no easy task. They desired him to dictate a commentary upon that most mystical of Old Testament writings the *Canticle of Canticles*. Thomas demurred saying that he had given up theological writing. The monks reminded him that their great St. Bernard had worked to the end, dictating even when dying. To this Thomas replied smiling, "Give me Bernard's spirit and I will do likewise."

Thomas finally gave way to their wishes and dictated his commentary on the Canticle. He continued until he felt the cold hand of death upon his shoulder. By that time he had reached the eleventh verse of the seventh chapter — the words "Come my beloved, let us go forth into the fields." At this point he was seized with faintness and could not proceed. After he had revived a little he asked Reginald to hear his confession. It was during this confession, Reginald testified before the commission that was investigating the life of Thomas to determine whether or not he could be canonized, that Aquinas revealed to him for the first time the angelic visitation he had received at the time of his temptation at Rocca Sicca. After receiving absolution Thomas asked for viaticum and, in imitation of his holy Father, St. Dominic, he asked that he be taken from bed and laid upon the floor sprinkled with ashes to receive the Sacrament in due humility. His request was granted for these were the middle ages and such a request would not have been considered a sign that he had lost his mind. The abbot, himself, brought the viaticum accompanied by the entire community in solemn procession. Before receiving the Lord whom he had so faithfully and capably served Thomas made this protestation: "I receive thee, the prince of my soul's redemption, and the viaticum of my pilgrimage, for whom I have studied, watched, and labored. Thee have I preached. Thee have I taught. Against Thee I have never spoken neither am I wedded to my own opinion. If I have held anything which is untrue, I subject it to the judgment of the Holy Roman Church, in whose obedience I now pass from this life." As he received the sacred host the saint uttered his favorite ejaculation: *"Tu es Christus, rex aeternae gloriae"* — *Thou art Christ the King of eternal glory*.

After the reception of Holy Communion Thomas made his thanksgiving in the words of the *Adoro Te*, the hymn which he himself had composed. The English translation which follows is a careful and faithful rendition of this beautiful poem although it does not quite catch the grandeur of the Latin original which is probably written at the same time as the office of the Feast of *Corpus Christi* as a possible substitute for one of the hymns contained therein.

O Godhead hid, devoutly I adore Thee
Who truly art within the forms before me;
To Thee my heart I bow with bended knee
As failing quite in contemplating Thee.

Sight touch and taste in Thee are each deceiv'd
The ear alone most safely is believ'd
I believe all the Son of God has spoken
Than Truth's own word there is no truer token.

God only on the Cross lay hid from view;
But here lies hid at once the manhood too;
And I, in both professing my belief
Make the same prayer as the repentant thief.

Thy wounds, as Thomas saw, I do not see;
Yet Thee confess my Lord and God to be;
Make me believe Thee ever more and more
In Thee my hope, in Thee my love to store.

O Thou memorial of our Lord's own dying!
O living bread to mortals life supplying!
Make Thou my soul henceforth on Thee to live
Ever a taste of heavenly sweetness give.

O loving pelican! O Jesus, Lord!
Unclean I am but cleanse me with Thy blood;
Of which a single drop, for sinners spilt,
Can purge the entire world from all its guilt.

Jesus! whom for the present veil'd I see,
What I so thirst for, oh, vouchsafe to me:
That I may see Thy countenance unfolding,
And may be blest Thy glory in beholding.

After he had received the viaticum Thomas returned to
the bed. He was still sinking, but slowly, and he still retained
the use of his faculties. During the day he was heard to repeat

frequently, "Soon, soon will the God of all comfort complete His mercies and fulfill my desires. Soon I shall be satiated in Him and drink of the torrent of His delights. I shall be inebriated in the abundance of His house, and in Him who is the source of life, I shall behold the light." Extreme Unction was administered to him the following day, March 6, 1274, and his mind still unclouded, Thomas responded himself to the prayers said by the priest.

After his reception of the last rites Thomas delivered a short exhortation to the Dominicans who were present who were still praying for his recovery. Reginald, in particular, could not seem to resign himself to the imminent loss. Reginald was somewhat a child of this world and he seems to have been a little imprudent at times. Always in the front of his mind was the idea that one day Thomas, like Bonaventure, would be forced by the Pope to accept the cardinal's hat and the faithful companion chose the most inopportune time to blurt out his hopes on this score. This was one of the occasions, the wrong one as usual, that Reginald decided to express his disappointment in not being a cardinal's companion. "O Father," he is reported to have said to the dying Thomas, "I had so depended on your going to the Council of Lyon and receiving a dignity which would have given great glory to the Order and to your own family." By "great glory" Reginald was referring to the cardinalate. Thomas chided his friend saying, "Take care, my son, not to admit such thoughts. What I have always asked of God, He has granted me by taking me out of this world as I am, and it is the subject of my thanksgiving. I might, indeed, have made more progress and been more useful to others but God in His goodness has made known to me that the reason why, without merit of mine, He has given light and grace at an earlier age than other doctors, was that He might mercifully shorten my exile and admit me the sooner to His glory. If you love me you will rejoice, for my consolation is perfect."

Thomas, who throughout his life had shown the courtesy and consideration of others that is characteristic of the saint, could not now on his deathbed, racked though he was with pain, forget the carefully cultivated habits of a lifetime. If there is one note that runs throughout the scene of his death it is that of saintly politeness. A courteous gesture was his last act. He thanked the Benedictines for their kindness to him in his last illness. Just before he died one of the monks asked him what is the best way to live without offending God. "He who walks in the presence of God and is always ready to give an account of his actions to Him certainly will never be separated from Him by sin." These were his last words. A short while later the last agony seized him and the man from Rocca Sicca returned his pure soul to its Creator a few minutes after midnight on March 7, 1274.

Chapter 22

Post Mortem

THE news of the death of Aquinas threw a pall over the University of Paris, the scene of his greatest battles and his most significant victories. The university realized that it had lost its greatest doctor, its most brilliant son, to whom more than to any other it owed its pre-eminence in theology and philosophy. Paris was not willing to relinquish its claim on its great professor even after death. The faculty of arts at the university, that faculty which had been but lately dominated by Siger of Brabant and his party, wrote to the Dominican chapter convened in Florence in 1274 a few months after the death of Thomas, and praised the merits of Aquinas in the most extravagant terms. They called him the beacon and the sun of the century, the most brilliant light in the Church, and they ended their eulogy with the petition that the remains of the great philosopher be given to the university. They pointed out that Paris had reared, nourished, and cultivated the great genius and that it would be entirely unfitting that he find his final resting place in any other city. The chapter refused to grant the request.

But if the faculty of arts at Paris was willing to bury the hatchet and acclaim Thomas as the university's greatest son that was, by no means, the attitude taken by the faculty of theology and Stephen Tempier, Bishop of Paris. To Tempier, the death of Aquinas seemed to mean one thing, a chance to proclaim him a heretic now that the brilliant mind and golden tongue were unable to raise an impregnable defense.

In 1277, three years after his death, Tempier condemned as heretical twenty-two Thomistic propositions. Tempier had been encouraged to take the step by the fact that another intransigent opponent of Thomas, the Dominican Robert Kilwardby had, a short while after being consecrated Archbishop of Canterbury on October 11, 1272, solemnly censured certain Thomistic propositions. And Kilwardby's animus had blinded him to the extent that he abused his episcopal privilege by granting an indulgence to all who would join him in condemning Thomas. Thus bolstered by a member of Thomas' own order, the heroic Tempier raised his snickersnee to decapitate his old enemy. The fact that he chose the anniversary of the saint's death to strike his blow is enough indication of the spirit in which it was delivered.

Yet if Tempier thought that he could strike Thomas with impunity he was as wrong as he was mean. The white knight of Christendom was indeed dead and could no longer mow down opponents with the sharp sword of his mind, but the old warrior to whom he had been esquire, the great fighter who had taught him the art of battle — he was very much alive. Albert the Great in his convent at Cologne heard of the proposed condemnation and determined that the cowardly Tempier would not desecrate the tomb of Thomas unchallenged. He would find at the door of that tomb a hoary-headed warrior ready and anxious to dispute his entry. As soon as he heard of Tempier's intention Albert set out for Paris, on foot as usual. The journey was a long one and Albert was seventy years of age, so the Dominicans at Cologne did their best to dissuade him from his purpose but to no avail, for the doughty fighter was determined.

Arrived at Paris Albert ascended the Dominican chair at the university and delivered a sermon on the text: What a glory it is for one who is living to be praised by the dead. Then with burning eloquence he eulogized the genius of Thomas to the professors of the university, who attracted by his great name, which, even then was almost legendary, had gathered to hear him. He gave a masterly discourse defending the writings of Thomas and the unquestionable sanctity of his life. He appealed to the professors to stand with him at this crucial moment to defend the name of their most illustrious confrère.

It cannot be said with certainty what effect Albert's plea had upon the professors. It would seem, however, that the response was not too enthusiastic for the bishop of Paris was not stayed in his efforts to revenge himself. The old man had been apparently beaten. At the age of seventy and wearied by his long trip his wit had not the hairspring quality it once possessed. Then, too, as provincial and bishop he had long been away from the intense study of theology. He had not been able to keep pace with the long strides of Thomas in his development of Aristotle's teaching. The gallant old man, despite his readiness to fight on behalf of his beloved son, must have realized that his best fighting days were behind him. Nevertheless as he left Paris, with sagging shoulders and bowed head to return to Cologne, even the enemies of Thomas must have admired him for his heroic effort.

On March 26, 1277, about three weeks after the condemnation at Paris the valiant Kilwardby, second to none as a ghost fighter, took a further stab at Thomas by publishing another condemnation of his writings. The Dominican bishop and his Parisian brother in the episcopate however, were not the only Church dignitaries who refused to allow Thomas to rest in peace. The Franciscan doctors were not quite ready to forgive him for disturbing their equilibrium while he was yet in this life. In 1282 the general chapter of the Friars Minor held in Strasburg placed the *Summa* on the list of books forbidden to be read in Franciscan schools.

But to the credit of the Order of Preachers, which had not given Thomas too militant a support during his life, let it be recorded that it did not forsake Dominic's greatest son in death. In 1278, in their general chapter held at Milan, the Dominicans passed a resolution to defend the writings of Aquinas. Shortly afterwards Thomism was adopted as the official teaching of the Order. In thus publicly proclaiming the orthodoxy of Thomism the Dominicans were anticipating the official decrees of the Church. Rome soon recognized that in Thomas God had granted the Church one of her greatest teachers and on July 18, 1323, the Church paid him the highest tribute when she raised him to the altars as St. Thomas Aquinas.

In proclaiming the sanctity of Thomas, John XXII declared, "Thomas alone has illuminated the Church more than all the other doctors together. . . . His philosophy can have proceeded only from some miraculous action of God." This put an end to all attempts to stigmatize Thomas as a heretic. Down through the centuries, and including his lifetime, the Popes have always been the finest friends and stanchest defenders of Aquinas. Sixty-five of them have pronounced favorably upon his teaching. Some of them have issued bulls backing that teaching with all the weight of papal authority and urging its universal adoption. In 1346, Clement VI exhorted the Order of Preachers never to deviate from his teaching. In 1406, Innocent VII officially confirmed the Thomistic doctrine as taught by the Dominicans. Pius V in 1567 proclaimed him Doctor of the Church and in 1570 he authorized an edition of all his writings. In 1594 Clement VIII recommended the Society of Jesus to adhere to Thomistic teaching. And on April 23, 1718, Clement XI gave solemn approbation to the Academy of Saint Thomas in Rome.

Notwithstanding all this papal approval Thomism was not adopted throughout the universal Church. A few of the orders, notably the Dominicans, the Carmelites, and the Benedictines, and an infrequent seminary elected to follow the teaching of St. Thomas. Scholasticism, says Maritain, "proceeded to squander its strength in futile rivalries and decadent systems." The scholastics outside of Thomism sank lower and lower and finally floundered. Philosophy became synonomous with captious hairsplitting and a parade of the powers of memory, until in the sixteenth century it had become the laughing stock of the world. The comic argument between the two gravediggers in Hamlet is a burlesque of a scholastic debate. With the dawn of the age of scientific discovery scholastic philosophy was in such disrepute that no one who had anything else to do bothered with it and the physical scientists in casting about for a philosophic system upon which to base their theories and explain the phenomena of unfolding nature never gave the system of the schools a second thought. And all this time Catholic seminaries and educational centers, passing Thomism by, were teaching decadent scholasticism or worse.

But this could not go on forever. The pearl of great price could not always remain buried beneath the rubbish heap of irrational systems of thought. Some day there would come upon the scene a man of energy and authority who would have the rubbish cleared away. It took the world six long centuries to produce that man. On the Feast of St. Dominic, August 4, 1879, Leo XIII, the greatest Pope of his own and the preceding century electrified the world with the encyclical *Aeterni Patris* in which he declared, "Now above all the Doctors of the Schools towers Thomas Aquinas, the leader and master of them all, who, as Cajetan observes, 'because he had the utmost reverence for the Doctors of antiquity, seems to have inherited in a way the intellect of all' . . . . He may be compared to the sun, for he warmed the world with the warmth of his virtues and filled it with the radiance of his teaching." Leo proclaimed Thomas the official teacher of the Church and by papal edict commanded that all Catholic institutions follow his system.

St. Thomas Aquinas had at last found a worthy champion. The Angel of the Schools had at last come into his own and his own had at last received him.